The Unmarried Mother

SHEILA TOFIELD WITH
JANE SMITH

PENGUIN BOOKS

PENGUIN BOOKS

Published by the Penguin Group

Penguin Books Ltd, 80 Strand, London WC2R 0RL, England

Penguin Group (USA) Inc., 375 Hudson Street, New York, New York 10014, USA

Penguin Group (Canada), 90 Eglinton Avenue East, Suite 700, Toronto, Ontario, Canada M4P 2Y3
(a division of Pearson Penguin Canada Inc.)

Penguin Ireland, 25 St Stephen's Green, Dublin 2, Ireland (a division of Penguin Books Ltd)

Penguin Group (Australia), 707 Collins Street, Melbourne, Victoria 3008, Australia
(a division of Pearson Australia Group Pty Ltd)

Penguin Books India Pvt Ltd, 11 Community Centre, Panchsheel Park, New Delhi – 110 017, India

Penguin Group (NZ), 67 Apollo Drive, Rosedale, Auckland 0632, New Zealand
(a division of Pearson New Zealand Ltd)

Penguin Books (South Africa) (Pty) Ltd, Block D, Rosebank Office Park,
181 Jan Smuts Avenue, Parktown North, Gauteng 2193, South Africa

Penguin Books Ltd, 80 Strand, London WC2R 0RL, England

www.penguin.com

First published 2013
001

Copyright © Sheila Tofield, 2013

Set in 12.5/14.75pt Garamond MT Std
Typeset by Jouve (UK), Milton Keynes
Printed in Great Britain by Clays Ltd, St Ives plc

ISBN: 978-1-405-91134-4

www.greenpenguin.co.uk

MIX
Paper from
responsible sources
FSC™ C018179
www.fsc.org

Penguin Books is committed to a sustainable
future for our business, our readers and our planet.
This book is made from Forest Stewardship
Council™ certified paper.

ALWAYS LEARNING   PEARSON

This is for Pat and Chris, who told me I should write a book, so I did. Also to Peter . . . to fill in the gaps

Love does not delight in evil but rejoices
with the truth.

It always protects, always trusts, always
hopes, always perseveres.

I

It's a complicated thing, love. You fall into it and out of it; find it in unexpected places, sometimes with unlikely people; you long to have it and to give it; and the having as well as the giving of it can make you do things you never thought you were capable of doing – both good things and bad. In all its many forms and guises, love can colour and control almost every aspect of our lives. It's only now, as I look back over my own life, that I realize the extent to which it moulded my character and informed every major decision I ever made.

For many years I was buffeted and swayed this way and that by love's presence or absence: by my mother's total lack of it for me; by thinking I'd been given it as a child and then having it snatched away when I needed it most; by falling into it, and out of it again; by being overwhelmed by it when my children were born; and by sharing it at last with a wonderful man who taught me, if not to love myself, at least to like the person I could see reflected in his eyes when he looked at me.

I'm eighty-one now – old enough to have learned a few things about life and not yet so feeble-minded that I don't realize I've forgotten more things than I can remember. Something I've known since I was a child, however, is that some things *are* what they *are*, so there's no point wishing they were something else, however tempting that might be.

Despite all this talk of love, I'm a practical, logical person, which is why I'm going to begin my story at the beginning, at the time when I was learning about the way things were and about the futility of wishing they were different.

My sister Mabel was a teenager when I was born, in February 1931. Mabel's father had died during the First World War, so my mother was a young widow with a little girl when she met her second husband, John (Jack) Edward Manns. My mother and Jack Manns had my older brothers, in ascending order of age, Harry, Eric, Bill and John; then there was a gap of six years before I was born; and two and a half years later – six months after Jack Manns died – my mother gave birth to the last of her children, Eddie.

If our house had caught fire at any time during my childhood and my mother could have chosen only one person or item to save from the flames, it would have been her boyfriend, Ernie Burns, if he'd been there; there's no question about that. If the fire had broken out at a time when Ernie Burns was at home with his wife, my mother would, probably, have rescued Eddie. Her next choice would have depended on whether the fire occurred before or after our move from Wellgate to Eastwood Lane and the purchase of the brown settee she was so proud of. I'd certainly have been last on any list, just after my sister Mabel. But, as I say, things are the way they are, and there's nothing to be gained from deluding oneself or from harbouring grudges about something like that – at least, not when you're an adult. A few delusions might have been nice when I was a child, though; or in my teens, when my mother told me an important and very unpalatable truth that changed who I'd always thought I was.

But I'm digressing. So I'll go back to the beginning.

Mabel was already married when Jack Manns died, which left my mother with five children under the age of twelve and another on the way. My mother had a tough life, and although I can't think of many good things to say about her, I do have to give her credit for the fact that she worked extremely hard. There was no welfare system in those days, and even by taking in other people's washing and ironing as well as going out to work cleaning offices and private houses, she barely earned enough to feed herself and her children.

I can remember one day, when I was quite young, my mother put a large brown-paper-wrapped parcel into my arms and told me to take it to a house up the road. The parcel was heavy and I had to keep moving it from side to side so that I could catch even a glimpse of the pavement ahead of me. When I knocked on the door of the house, the woman who lifted the parcel out of my aching arms laughed and said, 'I couldn't see you. I thought for a moment it had walked here all by itself.' Then she handed me half a crown to take home for my mother, which, although it would have bought quite a lot at that time, didn't seem very much money for washing and ironing all the clothes there must have been in such a big parcel.

Despite my mother's hard work, we were always very poor. For the first few years of my life, we lived in a small, one-up one-down house in Wellgate, in Rotherham, Yorkshire. The 'one-up' was a bedroom, where my mother slept with Eddie when he was a baby, after Jack Manns died. My bed was on the landing, tucked away in a corner opposite the wooden ladder my four older brothers climbed up to get to the two double beds they shared in the attic. I don't remember very much about that house, but one of the few vivid memories I do have is of getting up in the mornings and having to be careful where I put my feet so that I didn't tread on the horrible black beetles that scurried across the floor, over the hearth and up the curtains in the kitchen/living room.

At the back of the house there was a small paved yard, in the middle of which were stone steps leading up to the brick-built lavatory we shared with several neighbouring houses. The lavatory itself was a large, round, metal drum with a circular piece of wood on top of it – the sort of thing you might only find today on the most rustic of rural campsites. It was quite high and not easy for a child to reach, and every time I used it, I was terrified of falling into the disgusting, foul-smelling mess inside. There was no flush system: the contents of the lavatory were simply drained out at irregular and infrequent intervals. The appalling stench and the risk of disappearing into a quagmire of human waste meant that I always waited until the very last minute before making a dash for the loo, and I welcomed the occasions when someone was in there and my mother had to put a sheet of newspaper on the ground in the yard for me to squat down on instead.

On one occasion, when I was about four years old, I left it just a bit too long, and as I ran up the stone steps, I stumbled and fell, banging my eye on the step above me. Fortunately, I managed to pick myself up, open the wooden door of the privy and clamber on to the seat just in time to avoid a different sort of accident. Although my head was throbbing painfully and I was fighting back tears, at least I hadn't wet my knickers, which meant that my mother wouldn't have *that* reason to shout and swear at me and tell me how much she already had to do and how little she needed an idiot child who was of no use to man nor beast and who did nothing except create more work for her.

My mother had a vast store of idiomatic expressions to fit almost any and every occasion, including at least half a dozen that were directly related to what she considered to be my many and varied inadequacies. She often used to tell me angrily, as she pushed me out of her way, 'I don't know what's the matter with you, Sheila Manns. You haven't got the sense you were born with.' (In reality, she rarely spoke to me without swearing, but I've heard enough ugly words in my life not to want to repeat them now.) Sometimes, I didn't know what it was that I'd done wrong; when I did, I'd have a heavy feeling in my stomach because I believed that she was right and I *was* hopelessly stupid.

When I came out of the lavatory and went back into the house on the day I'd fallen, the front door was ajar and my mother was standing in the doorway talking to a woman who had stopped on the pavement outside. I knew better than to interrupt her, or to expect any sympathy for the pain that was filling my head. So I lay on my stomach on the settee in the kitchen/living room, pressed my face into a cushion and sobbed as quietly and unobtrusively as I could.

A minute or two later, when I lifted my hot, damp head to take a breath, I glanced down at the cushion and let out a yell that brought my mother instantly and furiously into the room.

'What the bloody hell's wrong with you now?' she shouted at me, towering above me with a clenched fist pressed against each of her hips and a belligerent expression on her face.

I held out the cushion to show her the blood and she put the open palm of her hand on the top of my head to tilt it towards the light so that she could examine the cut above my eye. As she cleaned my face and spread a liberal layer of boracic ointment over the wound, she told me again how stupid I was – for having fallen in the first place and then for soiling the cushion.

It was 1935, in the days before the establishment of the National Health Service, when the cost of a visit to a doctor or hospital for stitches – in fact, for anything other than to treat a life-threatening illness or injury – was beyond the financial means of families like ours, and certainly of a widow like my mother. So although the boracic ointment prevented the development of an infection in the wound above my eye, it left a scar when it healed, which still remains to this day.

When I was five years old, I used to visit a neighbour who lived a little way up the hill from our house and was always very kind to me. She'd give me a drink and talk to me and sometimes, when she was preparing a meal for her family, she'd let me help her peel the potatoes, which made me feel very grown-up.

One day, my mother told me, 'You're not to go up there any more.'

'But why, Mam?' I asked her. 'I don't get under anyone's feet and I always make sure I have the sense I was born with.' I didn't really know what that meant; it just seemed like a good thing to say in my defence because my mother was always telling me, in a rough, angry way, that the sense I was born with was something I *didn't* have. It clearly wasn't as persuasive an argument as I'd hoped, however, and she just repeated, more irritably this time, that I wasn't to go up there again.

I was heartbroken. I couldn't understand what could have happened and I couldn't even bear to consider the possibility that the neighbour had told my mother she didn't want me to go there again. Although I wasn't really frightened of my mother when I was a child, I rarely disobeyed her: she was short-tempered enough when I was doing exactly what I'd been told to do for me not to risk incurring her full-blown wrath by being deliberately naughty. On this particular occasion, my disappointment must have outweighed my instinct for self-preservation and when I was certain that she was safely out of earshot, I muttered defiantly to myself, 'I'm going to go up there anyway. She won't even know I've gone.'

7

It was a few days later when I ran up the hill again and knocked on the back door of the neighbour's house. When she opened it, she didn't smile at me with twinkling eyes or reach out to put her arm round my shoulder and draw me into the house as she'd always done before. She stood in the doorway, looking at me with a sad sort of face and said, 'You can't come in, pet. Your mother's told me I mustn't let you. I'm sorry, but you mustn't come here again.' Then she stepped backwards into the house and shut the door, and as I walked slowly down the hill towards home, everything in the world around me was blurred by my tears.

I'd learned to accept that my mother didn't want me at home; what I *couldn't* understand was why she didn't want me to go somewhere else, where I didn't get under people's feet and annoy them. Looking back on it now, of course, I realize that my mother decided to stop those visits purely and simply because she knew how much I enjoyed them.

Many years later, my sister Mabel told me about a similar thing that had happened when she was a little girl. She'd got up one morning and our mother had snapped at her, 'You needn't put your school clothes on. You're not going to school today.'

'Aren't I?' Mabel asked her. 'Why not?'

'Because you're going to your grandfather's funeral.' She sounded impatient, as if she thought Mabel should have known that her grandfather was being buried that day. But until that moment Mabel hadn't even known she *had* a grandfather. She had no memory of ever having met him, or any other member of her father's family, which at least meant that she wasn't upset to be told that he'd died.

As soon as Mabel was dressed, she set out to walk alone to the church where her unknown relative was to be buried. Fortunately, her father's family were very happy to see her and after the funeral they made a great fuss of her, telling her how delighted they were that she'd come and how lovely it would be if they could see her again.

She was invited back to visit her aunts, uncles and cousins several times after that day, and they were very kind to her. And then, one day, our mother told her, 'You're not going back there any more.' She didn't give a reason, and it wasn't until years later that Mabel discovered that the visits had been stopped out of spite and jealousy and because our mother couldn't bear anyone else but her to be the centre of attention. Mabel never saw her father's family again; she often wondered what excuse, if any, our mother had given them and if they'd been as hurt and disappointed as Mabel herself had been when the visits stopped.

I was a middle-aged woman when Mabel told me that, and other stories, too, about how our mother had treated her when she was a little girl. I wish we'd talked about it before then. Growing up knowing that your own mother doesn't love you makes it difficult to believe you're lovable.

In addition to seven full-term pregnancies, my mother had several miscarriages – not all of them as a result of natural causes – and she often told us, 'If only I'd known what I know now, *none* of you would have been born.'

It wasn't that she was incapable of loving anyone: she'd loved Ernie Burns for years and she continued to do so for many more. And because she loved him, the lives of her children had to revolve around him and what he wanted – as her own life did.

Ernie Burns worked shifts at Rotherham Forge and Rolling Mills and often spent his afternoons at our house. There were many occasions when Eddie and I got home from school, burst through the back door into what appeared to be an empty house and, a few minutes later, Ernie Burns would walk down the stairs, followed by my mother, who'd be patting her hair and straightening her apron. He didn't speak to us – he rarely did; he didn't even glance in our direction as he walked past us and out of the house to catch the bus home to his wife. As soon as he'd gone, my mother would snap at us irritably about something.

The same thing must have been happening when our older brothers were at school and it continued when they were working in the mines and steel mills. The strange thing was that we never talked to each other about it, not even when we were adults. I suppose it was a subject none of us wanted to discuss.

When I was five, I started going to Alma Road School in Rotherham. I'd been looking forward to it for months and I can remember walking there on the first day with my brother Harry, who went to a school on the opposite side of the playground. I didn't feel worried or anxious, just excited. I didn't have any clear understanding of what going to school would be like; I just knew that there would be other children there, that I'd be taught to read, and that I was going to love it. And I did.

I've always liked talking, to anyone and everyone – I did when I was five years old and I still do today – and when I walked into the classroom that first morning, there were more children there, which meant more people to talk to, than I'd ever seen in one place before. I was in my element and I joined in enthusiastically with everything we were told to do.

My mother's anger didn't ever build up gradually: it would always erupt suddenly without any warning and often without any cause that I could understand. That must have been why I didn't even notice my teacher's slowly but steadily increasing exasperation with me as I chattered my way cheerfully through every task we were set.

At an angle across one corner of the classroom there was a large blackboard on wheels, and when the teacher's patience finally wore so thin that it snapped, she called me out to the front of the class and pointed to the stool she'd positioned behind the blackboard. 'You will sit there until I tell you to go back to your desk,' she told me sternly.

The fact that it was supposed to be a punishment and an embarrassment was completely lost on me and I thoroughly enjoyed sitting at the front of the classroom, peering round the side of the blackboard whenever the teacher's back was turned and grinning at all my new friends. Clearly, my mother's constant criticism of me hadn't yet destroyed *all* my self-confidence!

Another wonderful thing about going to school, which I hadn't had any idea about before I started, was the food.

I loved school dinners. Almost all the other children would moan and complain about everything we were given to eat, but I never once grumbled about any of it. Compared to my mother's cooking, those meals were fantastic.

My two oldest brothers, Bill and John, were already going out to work by the time I started school. They worked in the coal mines – as their father, Jack Manns, had done – doing shifts from 6 a.m. to 2 p.m. or from 2 p.m. to 10 p.m. My mother cooked a meal every day and put a plate of food in the oven or on top of a saucepan of hot water on the stove to keep it warm for whichever of my brothers was still at work. It could be left like that for hours without there being any obvious detrimental effect, because my mother was a dreadful cook.

She only ever cooked three things that anyone would have eaten willingly: bread, custard tarts and Christmas cake. Actually, her Yorkshire puddings were good too, which was lucky because, as they were cheap and filling, we had them with almost everything.

Whenever my mother made a custard tart – which wasn't very often – she'd leave it on the cellar-head overnight and my brother Harry would always cut a slice to eat for his breakfast the next morning. When she discovered what he'd done, she'd fly into a rage and start shouting, 'What the bloody hell have you been doing with my custard tart? Who's taken a slice out of it? Who's had it?' The sound of her anger made me quake, but it didn't seem to bother Harry at all, or perhaps he felt that it was a price worth paying. She should have felt flattered: there wasn't much else she ever cooked that would have been stolen by anyone who wasn't in actual and imminent danger of starving to death.

The custard tarts and bread were at one end of the spectrum of my mother's culinary skills, and at the other end were the meals she cooked, which consisted of crucified meat accompanied by vegetables that had been boiled for so long they were virtually unrecognizable as food of any kind. We always had a joint of beef for Sunday lunch, which my mother put in the oven at the same time as she put a pan of potatoes on the stove to boil. When she eventually decided that it was time to eat – a decision that bore no relationship to how long the food would take to cook – the meat would be as dry and as black as the charcoal it tasted of, and the potatoes would have disintegrated into a soggy, barely edible mush.

When we'd eaten as much of our Sunday lunch as we could stomach, my mother would cut up any beef that was left over and put it into a pan of water with some carrots and onions. Then, as if it hadn't suffered enough, she'd boil it for hours to make a meal for the next day.

The only reason anyone ate anything my mother cooked was because if you didn't, you went hungry. It wasn't always an easy choice to make.

After I started having school dinners, I didn't need another meal when I got home and I'd just have bread and jam for my tea. Going to school was a wonderful thing!

2

My little brother Eddie was a spoilt pest in those days, which was a huge problem for me because I had to take him with me wherever I went. Whenever I turned my head, he was there beside me, impervious to my whining and pleading, 'Why can't you stay at home? Why do I always have to have you hanging around with me?' Just sometimes, it would have been nice to have been able to go out and play on my own. But that would have meant upsetting him, which was something my mother was never going to allow to happen to her favourite little boy, and it didn't matter where I was going or what I wanted to do, she'd always shout at me, 'You can't go without Eddie.'

One day when I was six, I was entertaining myself by jumping from the attic ladder on to my bed, climbing one rung higher after each jump and enjoying the thrilling sense of fear and the rapid beating of my heart as I launched myself across the floor.

It wasn't long before Eddie found me and as soon as he saw what I was doing, he decided he wanted to join in and jump too. Telling him he wasn't old enough, big enough or as clever as I was didn't discourage him, and I must admit that I was quite impressed when he jumped for the first time and managed to land safely on the bed. Then he did it again and it all went horribly wrong. As his body hit the floor, he cracked the back of his head on the bit of wood that was secured at the foot of the ladder to prevent it from sliding when people climbed up and down it, and suddenly there was blood everywhere.

My mother was furious with me, and while we were waiting for the ambulance to arrive to take Eddie to hospital, she shouted and swore at me and blamed me for having allowed him to join in with my game – as if *anyone* could have done *anything* to deter Eddie once he'd set his mind on something.

Fortunately, he didn't suffer any lasting harm as a direct result of his fall. Unfortunately, while he was in hospital he contracted diphtheria, which he passed on to Bill, Harry and me when he came home.

I must have been feeling very ill as we waited for the ambulance to come to our house again just a few days after it had come for Eddie – this time to take me and my brothers to the Badsley Moor Lane Fever Hospital. I can't think of any other explanation as to why I'd be sitting on my mother's knee: it was something I'd never done before, and I didn't ever do it again.

While we were waiting for the ambulance, my mother's mother, Grandma Pearson, arrived at the house. That was something else I don't remember ever happening before – the relationship between my mother and my grandmother wasn't close. When Grandma Pearson saw me sitting on my mother's lap, she sneered and called me 'a great big babby'. I was six years old, hot and damp with fever, my throat was sandpaper sore, and I was deeply hurt by the insult. Even my mother, who rarely showed any sign of sympathy for other people, was moved to mutter, 'Well, she's poorly' – although I think she said it more in her own defence than in mine.

At the fever hospital, I was separated from my brothers and taken to a girls' ward, but a couple of days later I was moved in with them, possibly in the hope that I'd be a comfort to Eddie. When Eddie had been infected with diphtheria during his previous visit to hospital, he'd become a carrier, and although he wasn't very ill, he missed our mother and cried almost incessantly. Unfortunately, putting my bed next to his cot didn't have the effect the nurses must have hoped it would, and they eventually tied a net over the top of Eddie's cot, which at least put an end to his repeated attempts to escape, although it had a less positive effect on his screaming.

After a few days, I began to feel better, but Harry remained seriously ill and Bill's condition continued to worsen until it became life-threatening. Diphtheria infected tens of thousands of people every year in the UK, and it killed thousands – about 3,000 people a year at that time, many of them children. When we were ill, a new antimicrobial drug had recently become available. Later, in 1940, a national immunization programme was set up, which reduced the number of deaths to fewer than ten a year, but it hadn't been introduced at that time and Bill was one of the lucky ones whose lives were saved by the new drug in those early days.

All the patients at Badsley Moor Lane had infectious or contagious diseases and visitors weren't allowed on to the wards. At visiting times, the parents of very sick children used to stand in the corridor outside the ward waving through the window, while those children who were well enough to get out of bed would cry as they touched their parents' fingers through the glass.

Harry, Bill and I had been too ill to see our mother when she came to the hospital on the first Sunday we were there. She never came again, and eventually I stopped looking for her every day at visiting time.

Eddie was the first of us to go home – much to everyone's relief; then Harry and then Bill. I stayed in the hospital for nine whole months. Apparently, the infection had spread from my throat to my nose and every time a swab test was done, it was positive for the presence of the bacteria that cause diphtheria. I'd become a carrier, and although I felt fine by the time my brothers went home, I could have passed the infection on to other people, as Eddie had done to us.

It seems terrible to me now to imagine a little girl of just six years old being left all alone in hospital for nine months without a single visit from her mother. And it *was* terrible, in some ways. It certainly didn't do anything to slow the decline of my already ailing self-esteem to know that, in all those months, my own mother couldn't spare the time even once to take the short bus ride from our house to the hospital to see me. Paradoxically, perhaps, those nine months turned out to be the best of my entire childhood.

I knew that I irritated my mother, although I didn't understand why and I did try really hard not to. The reality was that I was nothing more than a nuisance and an inconvenience to her – another mouth to feed, another body to clothe – and she had no interest in me or emotional attachment to me. She only ever spoke to me directly to issue an instruction or criticize something I'd done that I shouldn't, or hadn't done that I should. In the hospital, however, people talked to me and listened to me; everyone was nice to me and the nurses treated me with a kindness I'd never experienced before. So I didn't miss my mother at all – or any other member of my family. And that's much sadder than the fact that my mother didn't bother to come to see me.

After Harry and Bill went home, I was moved back into the girls' ward, where I had a bed next to the hatch in the wall that separated the ward from the nurses' office. At night, when all the other children had settled down to sleep, I would lie with my eyes wide open, unable to suppress a grin of excited anticipation, and wait for one of the nurses to put her head through the hatch and ask, in a conspiratorial whisper, 'Would you like a hot drink?' It made me feel special and it was the best moment of the day.

In those days, it was the nurses – overseen by strict, authoritarian matrons – who kept hospitals spotlessly clean, as well as doing all the other tasks involved in caring for their patients' health. And when I was well enough to get up every day, I was allowed to 'help' with the cleaning. Feeling very grown-up, I'd buff and polish the huge oak chest that stood in the corridor outside the door of the ward until you could see your reflection in its gleaming wood. Then I'd almost burst with pride and pleasure when one of the nurses made a great show of inspecting it before announcing, in a very serious voice, that 'Even matron couldn't find fault with that!'

I was proud, too, of being given the responsibility of distributing sweets to the other children. The parents who *did* visit their children often brought them sweets, which would be put into a large tin that I'd carry from bed to bed and thrust in front of each child as I instructed them imperiously to 'Take just one!'

During the whole time I was in hospital, I didn't have a single visitor, but I was happier there than I ever remember being before. Even Christmas was more fun than it would have been at Wellgate with my family, and when a nurse took me with her to fetch the Christmas decorations that were stored in a shed in the hospital grounds, I had a feeling I didn't recognize at the time; I know now that it was the feeling of belonging.

Once I felt well again, the only disappointing thing about being in hospital was that my brothers and I had been admitted on the day before the Coronation of King George VI on 12 May 1937. It wasn't so much the Coronation itself that I regretted missing; it was the party everyone had been talking about for weeks, and the gift of something called a 'Coronation mug' that was to be given to every child at my school, which I'd been looking forward to, even though I didn't really know what it was, and which I never did receive.

I think I'd have been happy to stay in the hospital forever: I had other children to talk to and the nurses were kind to me and never made me feel that I was stupid or a nuisance. But I *was* happy when a nurse told me one day,

'I've got some great news for you, Sheila: you're going home today!' I'd been in hospital for so long by that time I could barely recall what life had been like at home, and I was excited at the prospect of seeing my family again. Clearly, it wasn't an excitement shared by my mother and, despite having received the postcard sent to her by the hospital telling her when to come to collect me, she didn't turn up.

I sat on the little chair by my bed, at first chattering away to anyone who'd listen, and then just waiting, silently. We didn't have a telephone at home – no one in our neighbourhood did in those days – and as there was no other way anyone could get in touch with my mother, after I'd been waiting for what felt like hours, I walked out of the hospital clutching the hand of a nurse and clambered into the back of an ambulance, which delivered me home to my family.

My mother didn't say a single welcoming word to me, or show any sign at all of being glad to see me – after I'd been in hospital for thirty-six weeks. It felt as though the nurses had become more of a family to me than my real family had ever been.

Not very long after I'd returned home, we moved from Wellgate to live in a house a few streets away, in Eastwood Lane. The back-to-back I'd lived in since I was born was in effect little more than a slum, and now, together with all the neighbouring houses, it was going to be demolished and we were being rehoused. Having few possessions and almost no furniture became a good thing on the day we trudged through the streets carrying everything we owned from our old house to the new one. I trailed behind, concentrating hard on trying to prevent my doll's pram from tipping over with the weight of the large oval mirror my mother had dumped on top of it, and ignoring my brother Eric's increasingly exasperated commands to 'Hurry up, Sheila, for pity's sake. If you walk any more slowly, you'll be going backwards with that damn thing.'

It was all worth it though: our new house was bigger and better than the old one in every respect. And it had its *own* lavatory, which was in a block of four in the backyard. We still had to cut up newspaper into little squares and hang it on the back of the door to use as loo paper, but having the day's news imprinted on your bottom was no price at all to pay for living in such a wonderful house and for the huge step up in the world that we'd very clearly taken.

People rarely remain satisfied with anything for very long, of course, and a few years later, when Eddie and I were in our teens, we often lamented the fact that we didn't live in one of the houses that were rented out by the council and that had their own bathrooms – inside – with modern, built-in baths complete with hot and cold running water. It was a yearning that was only heightened for me when Eddie's lovely girlfriend, Iris, invited me home to the house she lived in with her parents to have tea and then a bath in their luxurious bathroom. There were many reasons to like Iris and to be delighted when she and Eddie subsequently married, but that invitation had certainly helped to make me feel very well disposed towards her!

The front door of the house in Eastwood Lane was

kept locked, except on special occasions, and we used the back door, which was accessed via the passageway at the side of the house and which opened directly into the kitchen/living room. There was another room downstairs, at the front of the house, but it was kept 'for best' – which in reality meant that it was almost never used. Everything we did, from washing in the stone sink with its cold tap, to cooking on the kitchen range and eating at the scrubbed-wood kitchen table, we did in the kitchen/living room.

Built into a corner next to the sink was a copper for heating water, which was warmed – in the same way as the oven in the kitchen range – by piling hot coals from the open fire on to the grate underneath it. On washdays, my mother would build up the fire under the copper and then fill it with bucket after bucket of water from the cold tap. When the water was hot enough, she'd ladle it into the washtub, which was stored in the second cellar, next to the coal cellar, and which she'd already have rolled outside and pushed into position next to the heavy, iron-framed mangle.

She did the same thing every week on every washday, whatever the weather. Even when it was snowing, she'd stand outside in the yard, her hands swollen and almost purple, vigorously rubbing sodden clothes up and down the metal ridges of the washboard and then turning the handle that rotated the wooden rollers of the mangle and squeezed out all the surplus water. Sometimes the clothes would be stiff with ice within minutes of being pegged out on the washing line that hung across the yard.

I can't find it in my heart, even now, to feel much sympathy for my mother, but I do sometimes think about those washdays as I push my washing through the open door on the front of an automatic washing machine, or pull it out again and carry it a few steps across the tiled floor of the laundry room to the tumble dryer.

Above the open fire in the kitchen/living room was a mantelpiece on which my mother draped a length of tasselled cloth and arranged two china dogs, one at each end, from where they sat facing each other like sentinels of some ancient tomb – or, in this case, like guardians of the alarm clock that stood between them. Some years later, after Eddie had left school and was working as an apprentice with a firm of decorators, he replaced that mantelpiece with a lovely carved wooden one, wallpapered the room and painted the heavy, old-fashioned sideboard a very nice and, at that time, modern, grey colour.

Upstairs there were two bedrooms. Into the bigger room at the back of the house had been squeezed two double beds, which were shared by my brothers, and a single bed, where I slept. Into the much smaller bedroom at the front, my mother had somehow managed to cram a large bed, a dressing table and a tallboy.

Eddie started school not long after we'd moved to Eastwood Lane and every morning my mother would light the coal fire in the kitchen before shouting up the stairs to us to get up. She'd already have left for work by the time Eddie and I came down, and after we'd washed and got ourselves ready for school, I'd cut two slices of bread and spread them with jam for our breakfast. Sometimes, on particularly cold mornings, I'd ask Eddie, 'Shall we not bother to wash?' and he'd always laugh and say, 'Shall we not?' It was about as naughty as we dared to be.

Our mother would usually be at home by the time we got back from school in the afternoons. We'd barely have walked in through the back door before she'd be shouting at us to get out from under her feet and go outside, and we'd tumble out of the house again and join all the other children who were playing in the yards or in the streets.

Another way she used to get rid of Eddie and me was by sending us to stay at weekends with my sister, Mabel, and her husband, Bill. Mabel was nineteen (and I was three) when she got married. At first, she and Bill rented a couple of rooms and then they moved into a house in Hellaby, a small rural town just a short, thruppence ha'penny bus ride from the centre of Rotherham.

My mother never gave them a penny piece for looking after us, not even when they had three young children of their own. Luckily – for my mother as well as for Eddie and me – Bill was a kind man and he didn't complain about having us there or about the fact of having two extra mouths to feed for two days out of every seven when he could barely afford to feed and clothe his own family. It must have been very hard for Mabel and Bill.

For as long as it lasted, having somewhere like that to go to at the weekends was a blessing for me. My sister and her husband were very good to us and never once made us feel unwanted or a burden – which was the way I always felt at home with my mother.

My mother had two sisters, Gerty and Marion, and another place I loved visiting when I was a child was my

Auntie Marion's house. Auntie Marion had married a chimneysweep and become Mrs Shakespeare, and she and her husband had several children, including a son with an extraordinary talent for playing the piano. She was about as different from my mother and grandmother as it was possible to be, and although my mother rarely visited my grandmother, she did get on well with Auntie Marion – I think everyone did.

My mother used to tell a funny story about the time when she was visiting her sister and three of the children started quarrelling amongst themselves. Marion reprimanded them and then said, with what was supposed to be stern finality, 'You'll see two bonnie faces in heaven in a minute if you don't behave yourselves.'

'There are three of them,' my mother said.

'Ah yes,' her sister replied. 'But I've got to keep one of them to run the errands.'

It made my mother laugh whenever she told it. And it made me laugh too, although the most astonishing part of the story to me was the fact that Auntie Marion told her children off by saying something so mild, and without swearing. As I say, she was very different from my mother.

I was eight when my brother Eric announced that he'd joined the Navy; it was the most exciting thing that had happened since the day we'd moved house.

John and Bill both started working in the steel mills when they left school, and Eric got a job in the coal mines. Eric hated his job, and despite the fact that enlisting in the Navy for twelve years was a huge, life-changing decision to have made, it offered him what he knew might be his only means of escaping from spending the next thirty or forty years down the pit. To Eric, almost anything would have been better than that.

He hadn't mentioned to our mother what he was planning to do, or even that he had any interest in the Navy at all, and she was beside herself with rage when he came home and told her he'd signed up. Eric was more than old enough to make his own decisions, and my mother didn't care what any of us did anyway, as long as whatever it was didn't interfere with what *she* wanted to do – which made it difficult to understand why the news elicited in her as much fury as it did.

In fact, my mother and Eric had a furious argument every week on payday, because Eric always opened his own pay packet before he got home and my mother would shout at him in a harsh, ugly voice, 'How many times do I have to tell you? *I* will open your pay packet and *I* will decide how much I need and how much of it you can keep.'

On this occasion, she shouted and swore at Eric, while Eddie and I quaked, and then Eric said, 'I don't understand, Mam. I didn't think you'd be bothered. I don't understand what difference it makes to you if I'm down the pit or sailing the seven seas. Whereas it certainly makes a difference to me – the difference between being miserable for the rest of my life and having the chance to do something I want to do.'

After more yelling and cursing, the reason for my mother's fury finally became clear: it wasn't the prospect of Eric's departure from the bosom of his loving family that had upset her; it was the fact that she'd be losing the large proportion of his wages she took every week.

'But I'll still give you money,' Eric told her. 'I know it's hard for you, so although I'll be away, I'll send money to you every week.'

Suddenly, her anger evaporated, the shouting stopped, and the prospect of losing her son to the Navy became much easier for my mother to bear.

Eric left Rotherham shortly after that and we didn't see him again until he came home on leave. I was very proud of the way my brother looked in his uniform and I was sad when he announced that he was being sent to China and didn't expect to be home again for two whole years.

It was 1939 and, for many people, life was about to change.

3

On 1 September 1939, Hitler invaded Poland. Two days later, Britain and France declared war on Germany.

I was eight years old and the outbreak of war had little immediate impact on my day-to-day life, except that my school closed for a couple of weeks and we did some lessons at the YMCA until it opened again. Then, for Eddie and me at least, everything seemed to settle down into a new, not very different, normality.

For my older brothers John and Bill too, life continued pretty much as before. John was twenty at the start of the war and Bill was nineteen. They'd both been working in a steel rolling mill since leaving school at the age of fourteen, and as the jobs they were doing were considered to be vital, they were exempt from the call-up and they continued to work in the mill throughout the war. Eric had already joined the Navy earlier that year, as soon as he turned eighteen. He didn't go to China, as he'd expected to do; instead, his ship was sent to the Mediterranean and we didn't see him again for five years. Harry was fourteen at the start of the war and had already left school to work at Steel, Peech and Tozer, a huge steelworks in the Sheffield suburb of Tinsley. So he wasn't called up until later in the war, when he joined the Army and went out to Malaya.

The radio became a major focus of the lives of many people in Britain during the war. There was a special sort of silence that descended whenever a group of people stood in a shop, or wherever else they happened to be, and listened to the news bulletins that were broadcast throughout the day on the BBC Home Service. There was no mistaking the voices of the BBC newsreaders: they all spoke 'the King's English' and had identical, clipped tones. In fact, because they all sounded the same, it was thought that it would be a simple matter for the Germans to imitate them and broadcast false news reports. So, for the first time ever, the BBC employed a newsreader with a regional accent – an actor and Yorkshireman called Wilfred Pickles. It would have been a very clever foreigner who'd managed to imitate an accent that most British people outside of Yorkshire could barely understand!

Half the country's adult population listened to those news broadcasts, although they contained little in the way of detailed news, because we all knew that Hitler was listening to them too. The names of the towns that had been bombed in air-raids weren't mentioned, the numbers of casualties or fatalities were never revealed, and weather forecasts were dropped completely, as was any mention of the weather in any context, in case the information could be used to assist enemy planes.

Barrage balloons were raised above Clifton Park, where we often played as children, and anti-aircraft guns were set up at various sites around the town. Rotherham itself escaped relatively unscathed from German bomb attacks and suffered just two serious raids. The first was on the night of 19 August 1940, when there were two fatalities; the other was ten days later, on 29 August, when no one was reported to have been killed. Incendiary bombs *were* dropped on the town later that same year, however, during what became known as the Sheffield Blitz.

Less than ten miles away from Rotherham, Sheffield had a population at that time of just over half a million and was the site of numerous important heavy industries, including steel and armaments. So it was inevitable that it would be a prime target for attacks by the German Luftwaffe. The blitz that affected Sheffield took place over two cold, clear nights in December. The attack on 12 December was aimed at the city centre and surrounding residential areas; it began just after 7.30 p.m. and continued until four the next morning. The second raid, on 15 December, was shorter, lasting about three hours, and its focus was the city's major steelworks. At least 660 people were killed on just those two nights, another 1,500 were injured and 40,000 were made homeless.

I think it must have been the night of the second of the two raids on Sheffield when we heard the loud, low drone of planes flying overhead. My mother opened the rarely used front door, and Eddie and I stood with her in the doorway watching beams of light criss-crossing above us as they searched the skies for enemy planes.

We hadn't been standing there for very long when there was a terrific explosion. The air was still full of the sound of it when it felt as though massive shockwaves were shaking the ground underneath our house. We found out later that a bomb dropped by a German bomber had landed at the far end of Eastwood Lane – presumably short of its intended target in Sheffield.

We were still standing huddled together in the doorway when an air-raid warden came running down the road and shouted to my mother, 'Get inside! Get those children down into the cellar!' We shouldn't have needed to be told not to stand in the doorway gawping at enemy bombers flying low overhead, and it was an instruction he didn't have to repeat. Now that the planes had gone, the sky was lit by the eerie, red-orange glow of flames, the night seemed to reverberate with the sound of sirens and urgent voices, and my heart was racing as we scurried down into the cellar to wait for the all-clear. During the war, no one ever went to bed at night certain of what the next day would bring.

Food rationing affected everyone and many hours were spent standing patiently in queues. Until he left school, it was the job of my brother Harry to do the main, weekend shop; and then it became mine. I was only nine, and my head was spinning as I clutched the ration books and followed him round all the different shops while he explained what I'd have to buy every week in each one.

My mother used to buy meat at two local pork butchers, Andrassy's and Schonhut's, and early on at least one morning every week, after she'd already gone to work, I'd join the queue at one of them and wait in line, for what always seemed like hours, until she came to take my place. Then I'd run all the way to school so that I wouldn't be late. It was worth it, though, for the chance of getting some cold roast pork or potted beef, both of which were delicious in a bap or sandwich.

Sometimes, I'd be sent by my mother to join another long queue at a greengrocer's shop where they sold rabbits. As the only girl in the house after Mabel left home (when I was three), I was at the very bottom of the pecking order, which meant that when my mother made a rabbit stew, I was only ever given the ribs, which had almost no meat on them at all. But all these years later, I've tasted very few things better than Yorkshire pudding and rabbit gravy.

My mother also used to send me to Billie's fish and chip shop, which was open every lunchtime and evening, except on Sundays. The owner – the Billie after whom the shop was named – was a man in his thirties who, for some reason, wasn't called up, and who must have made a small fortune during the war years.

Although fish wasn't rationed, it wasn't always available – the movement of commercial fishing vessels in the North Sea was restricted during the war, many of them were requisitioned and many fishermen were called up. When the fryer *was* on, the queue always stretched from the shop counter, out through the door and on to the pavement. Everyone said that Billie's fish was fantastic; however, I can only vouch for the chips, which we had for lunch every Saturday, accompanied by a sausage for those of my brothers who were working.

One day, my mother gave me some raw liver wrapped in brown paper and said, 'Take this to Grandma Pearson. It'll do for her dinner.' We rarely saw my mother's mother – I don't remember ever visiting her at her house in Wellgate on any other occasion – and it was unusual for my mother to do anything for her at all.

When I arrived at my grandmother's house and walked in through the open back door, she was standing on the cellar steps, glancing up occasionally towards the light and hacking away with a little axe at the heel of a shoe. As any child will tell you, adults do some very peculiar things, but even for someone as old as my grandmother, who must have been in her late seventies at the time – younger than I am now – it seemed to be a particularly odd thing to be doing.

As I stood watching her, the words 'the terrible effects of poisonous gas' came into my mind. It was something people often talked about, in the hushed tones they used whenever they discussed the 'unspeakable things' that were all that could be expected from 'a man like Hitler'. We'd all been issued with gas masks, which we were supposed to carry with us at all times, and although I'd never been very clear about *how* Hitler was going to fill the air with poisonous gas, I did wonder if he might have decided to start doing it at my grandmother's house. I was still pondering the possibility when Grandma Pearson said, 'Have you come here because you wanted to stand gawping with your mouth open or did you want something?'

'What are you doing?' I asked her at last.

She glanced down at the shoe, then back up at me and said, in a voice that seemed to imply grave suspicions about my mental capacity, 'I'm cutting the heel off my shoe. It's too high, so I'm trying to make it lower.'

She was very pleased with the raw liver though.

*

I hated the blackout during the war. Even when the whole of Rotherham was plunged into darkness, my mother would still send me out on errands. I was afraid of getting lost and I'd walk along the pavement with one hand outstretched and in permanent contact with the front walls of the houses I was passing. It can't have been a completely overwhelming fear, however, because I managed to overcome it when there was something I really wanted to do, such as go to the cinema with my friend after school to see the film *The Wolf Man*.

Before the war, there were just a few hours of television programmes every day and only about 20,000 television sets in the entire country – none of which was owned by anyone we knew. On the day war was declared, all television broadcasting stopped – so that enemy aircraft couldn't use the transmissions as a beacon to guide them to London – and it didn't start again until 1946. In reality, television – its presence or absence – had no impact on the lives of most people because everyone went to the cinema.

Several of the big-name actors of the day were in *The Wolf Man*, including Lon Chaney Jr, Claude Rains and Béla Lugosi. Even so, I can't imagine why two ten-year-old girls would have wanted to see a horror film, or why we were allowed into the cinema on our own. The film would seem very tame and dated today, but at the time it really was very frightening – for adults, let alone for two little girls. My friend and I sat throughout almost the entire film with our hands in front of our faces, only occasionally daring to open our fingers and look through the gaps.

By the time we left the cinema it was dark, and I was

the only one who had a torch. My friend clutched my arm and pleaded with me, 'Please, Sheila, come with me. I can't go home on my own in the dark.' So I agreed to walk with her.

Except in the depths of the remotest countryside, it's never completely dark: even without the general light pollution produced by large towns and cities, there's always light from a house or a street lamp. On a cloudy night during the blackout, however, you could be on a street lined by houses and the only light you could see would be the small, nervously darting beam of your own torch.

After my friend had scuttled up the steps to her front door, I turned and walked quickly back the way we'd just come. Although I was trying very hard not to think about werewolves, lines of the verse that was repeated throughout the film kept coming into my mind:

> Even a man who is pure in heart
> And says his prayers by night
> May become a wolf when the wolfbane blooms
> And the autumn moon is bright.

I didn't know what wolfbane was; I just hoped it wasn't blooming that night.

I'd turned into Eastwood Lane and was nearly home when I heard a man's voice from behind me ask, 'Do you live round here?' I nearly jumped out of my skin. I thought I was going to faint, but somehow I managed to keep breathing – from just the bits of the film I'd seen through parted fingers, I knew, in graphic detail, what happened to girls who fainted in the dark.

I spun round just as the man caught up with me and fell into step beside me as I scurried along the pavement. Apparently oblivious to my distress, he kept asking me questions, to most of which I was unable to give coherent answers. By the time we reached my house, I was certain he must be able to hear the thudding of my heart.

'I live here,' I told him, turning away from him at last and feeling relief begin to flood through my veins like warm water. And then he reached out his hand, curled his fingers around my wrist, and the water turned to ice.

'Oh, don't go,' he said. 'Why don't you . . .' That's all I heard; I'd already snatched my arm out of his grip and was stumbling down the passageway towards the back door of our house, the beam from my little torch flashing around me like the light from a demented firefly.

My mother was in the kitchen/living room when I burst through the door. When I could breathe enough for her to understand what I was saying, she rushed out of the house, shouting and swearing in a way that would have made the man very afraid if he hadn't already disappeared into the night.

Despite my mother's threats to 'tear the effing bastard limb from limb if I ever clap eyes on him round here again', she had no sympathy for me. She told me I was stupid and that what had happened was my fault – for reasons that didn't make much sense to me at the time and which I can't remember now. And she continued to send me out on errands in the dark.

*

Physical abuse by a parent is a terrible thing. As well as causing actual bodily injury, it results in emotional damage that can last throughout an entire lifetime. Psychological abuse can't kill a child – at least, not directly – but it can have very marked and long-lasting effects on self-esteem, self-image, confidence, behaviour and expectations about life. If a child grows up believing that he or she is stupid and unlovable, the potential is created for a lifetime spent making wrong choices based on a very powerful and previously unrequited need to be loved. As a child, I may have had to accept that things *are* what they *are*; I wonder if what happened later, however, was the result of wanting to believe they were different and that I *was* lovable, despite what my mother always told me.

One morning, my teacher called out my name when she was taking the register and I missed answering. Perhaps I was talking at the time, which I can see might have annoyed her, although I don't think it would have warranted her reaction, which was to hit me up and down my arms repeatedly with a ruler until the skin was covered with angry red welts.

When she stopped hitting me, she handed me a note and said, 'As there's clearly nothing taking place in the classroom that you feel is worthy of your attention, you can take this to my house and give it to my husband.'

I was very offended: first she'd hit me and now she was going to make me trudge through the streets of Rotherham on some private errand for her. I didn't say anything though – you didn't argue with adults in those days and you certainly didn't say 'no' to a teacher. I set off with the note in my hand and indignation leaking like steam from my ears.

It turned out to be a long walk to the teacher's house, which took me past the end of Eastwood Lane, and I decided to tell my mother what had happened. When I ran up the passageway at the side of our house, she was doing the washing in the yard.

'Look, Mam!' I said. 'Look what my teacher did to me!'

My mother barely glanced at my outstretched arms. 'Serves you right,' she snapped. 'You must have been doing something wrong. Get out the way. Can't you see I'm busy?'

I should have known better than to hope for sympathy from someone who hit me with her hand when she was mildly irritated and with a belt when she was really cross. I continued on my way, found my teacher's house, handed the note to her husband and only just got back to school in time for lunch, having missed the entire morning session of lessons.

'Sheila Manns's unpaid postal delivery services' aside, I did like school, although I always looked forward to the summer holidays, when I'd often go with a group of other children from the neighbouring houses to Listerdale Wood – always accompanied by Eddie, of course. It was a short bus ride away from where we lived and my mother was happy to give Eddie and me the ha'penny bus fare to get us out of the way for a few hours. I'd make jam sandwiches, fill a bottle with water from the tap in the kitchen and we'd be gone for the whole day, playing hide-and-seek and running through the trees as if we'd been released from cages.

One day, I decided it would be a good idea to take a wrap of cocoa powder, some sugar, milk and matches and build a fire in the woods to make a cup of hot chocolate. Unfortunately, it turns out that there's rather more to being a character from *Swallows and Amazons* than I'd thought, and I couldn't get the sticks to light. So there was no cocoa, which was disappointing, but at least it meant that Listerdale Wood wasn't razed to the ground by a raging fire!

Another place we used to go was Clifton Park, where the barrage balloons were tethered during the war. Getting there seemed to involve walking up every single hill in Rotherham – of which there are many. It was worth it though.

The park had originally been the estate of Clifton House, which was built for a wealthy industrialist in the eighteenth century and bought a century later by the Municipal Borough of Rotherham, who turned it into a museum. During the war, the council organized all sorts of games, shows and concerts in the park and I went with friends – and the ubiquitous Eddie – to lots of the events that took place there in the school holidays.

The love of reading that made me want to re-enact a scene from *Swallows and Amazons* or *Five on a Treasure Island* that day in Listerdale Wood is something I've retained all my life, and as a child I made regular visits to the local library. Reading wasn't something that was either instigated or encouraged by my mother. In fact, the sight of me sitting reading a book used to incense her and she'd often remark angrily, 'You've got your nose in a book again! I can find something useful for you to do if you've got time to waste.'

I already had a lot of chores to do, and I did almost all of the housework in the school holidays. One of my jobs was cleaning the two stone steps and doorstep outside the front door. Although they were seldom used, they had to be regularly dampened with a wet cloth and then scrubbed with a donkey stone. Everyone used donkey stones in the 1930s and 1940s – at least, everyone in our neighbourhood did. They were scouring blocks made from a dried-out paste of pulverized stone, cement, bleach powder and water. Used originally in the textile mills in the north of England to remove grease from steps and give them a non-slip finish, they soon became an essential element in the cleaning kit of every northern housewife for scouring and enhancing the natural yellow-ochre colour of domestic stone steps. I don't suppose anyone still uses them today, now that there are so many cleaning products available that don't require the application of exhausting amounts of 'elbow grease'.

From the age of eleven, it also became my job to cook the Sunday lunch. Every Sunday morning, my mother would go to work and then to the pub with Ernie Burns, and lunch had to be ready when she got home at 2 p.m. With no one to tell me any differently, I followed her instructions and produced the same burnt offering and watery mush she'd always made. Then I went to secondary school, started doing cookery lessons and discovered a whole new way to prepare food that was not only a revelation to me but also a source of considerable appreciation on behalf of every member of my family.

Something else I found out during those cookery lessons at school was that not everyone cooked on an old range with a cracked oven that was heated by coals and that, while it might have smoked a fish to perfection, rendered an apple pie almost inedible. My secondary school had the first modern gas ovens I'd ever seen, and I eventually summoned the courage to suggest to my mother that we should pay a visit to the gas showroom in town, just to have a look. A few days later, we took delivery of a brand new, state-of-the-art gas cooker, and cooking the Sunday dinner stopped being the laborious chore it had always been.

4

Having failed the eleven-plus, I went to Spurley Hey Secondary Modern School in Rotherham, rather than to the more academically orientated grammar school. My favourite subjects were English and History and my least favourite was Laundry – which, in 1942, wasn't a lesson the boys had to take part in, of course!

It was shortly after I'd started at the secondary school that I developed a passion for knitting. You could buy knitting patterns for almost anything – from sweaters, cardigans and twinsets to waistcoats, skirts and slippers – and it wasn't long before I was doing very difficult Fair Isle patterns, which were all the rage at the time. I'd often take my knitting into school so that I could do it during the lunch break, and one day my teacher asked me what I was making. I was knitting the back of an intricately patterned Fair Isle jumper and when I showed it to her, she turned it over in her hands and exclaimed, 'The reverse side is as neat as the front of it! How on earth do you weave in all those different coloured wools without tangling them up into knots? It's beautiful, Sheila. Will you make one for me? I'll buy the wool, and I'll pay you, of course.'

My cheeks literally glowed with pride. I wasn't used to praise. I didn't expect to be good at things, which is why it hadn't been a surprise – to me or to my mother – when I'd failed the eleven-plus. I'd lived all my life with my mother's criticism and disapproval, and it had become the norm. So being praised by my teacher was even more gratifying than it might otherwise have been.

When we lived in Wellgate, I used to hear the woman who lived next door talking to her children in a way my mother never talked to us. Mrs Noble called people 'Flower', and every time I heard her say it, I'd feel envious and long for her to say it to me. Then, one day, I pushed open the wooden door of the lavatory in the yard just as she came out of her back door holding a basket of washing against her hip and she beamed at me and said, 'Ooh, it's you, Flower. I wondered who was in there.'

Sometimes when you've built something up in your mind and longed for it to happen and it finally does, it can be a bit disappointing. But being called 'Flower' by Mrs Noble was even better than I'd imagined it would be. Isn't that funny: that something as simple as that could make a little girl so happy? It puts into context, perhaps, how I felt when I was praised for something I'd actually *done*. And when I'd knitted a jumper for my teacher, other people asked me to knit things for them too, and I began to earn some pocket money.

After Winston Churchill became prime minister in 1940, he was very keen on 'establishing a state of society where the advantages and privileges which hitherto have been enjoyed only by the few, shall be far more widely shared by the men and youth of the nation as a whole'. They were words that sowed the seeds for the 1944 Education Act and for the government's post-war programme of 'social reconstruction' – and they were to have a direct effect on my life.

It was the desire to provide more opportunities for better education for the masses, combined with a shortage of teachers after so many young men – and women – had lost their lives in the war, that led to a decision to give children who had failed the eleven-plus a second chance to go on to further education. The selection of pupils was made by the staff of schools like mine and when I was thirteen I was told that I was one of the lucky ones who'd been chosen to go in front of a panel of judges for an interview.

I couldn't believe I'd been chosen, although I'd been working hard and doing well at school, particularly in arithmetic; and there was another reason too, as the teacher who'd recommended me explained.

'I was on duty in the playground the other morning,' she told me. 'You were sitting on a bench, writing away as if your life depended on it. You kept it up throughout the whole of break time. I was very impressed.'

I blushed and looked down at my feet. This time though, it wasn't the teacher's praise that brought the colour to my cheeks. I knew immediately which break time she was talking about and I didn't think what I'd actually been doing was something she'd approve of. I loved listening to the radio and singing along lustily to all the popular songs, and as soon as the other girls at school found out that I knew the words to the latest hits, they asked me to write them down for them. And that's what I'd been doing in the playground on the morning when my teacher had seen me and had then been instrumental in changing the course of my education, and probably of the rest of my life too. It's strange how so many things happen simply by chance: being in the right place at the right time, making a decision that sets in motion a whole chain of events or takes you down one particular path rather than another.

My mother just shrugged when I told her I was being put forward for the next stage in the process of selecting children to go to the grammar school. Despite her indifference, I was proud of being picked, and when the day of the interview arrived, I took a deep breath, wiped the damp from the palms of my hands on to my skirt and stepped forward to stand in front of the panel of judges.

I tried very hard to think of good answers to all the questions they asked me – which were mostly about myself and the things I liked doing. And then it was just a matter of waiting. After the interview, one of my teachers asked how I thought it had gone.

'They asked me if I had any hobbies,' I told her. 'So I was glad about the knitting.'

'Oh! You um . . .' Her hand flew to her mouth. 'You didn't tell them you were knitting something for me, did you?'

'Yes,' I answered. 'Oh dear, was that the wrong thing to say?' I could actually feel my heart sinking. It had seemed such a straightforward question when they asked it, perhaps the most straightforward of all of them. If I'd got *that* wrong, I had very little chance of getting a place at the grammar school.

'No. No, of course it wasn't the wrong thing to say,' the

45

teacher said hastily, with a smile that wasn't as reassuring as she probably hoped it would be. 'It's fine. It's just that . . .' She gave a nervous laugh. 'Well, the thing is . . . I wouldn't want anyone to think I was exploiting you.'

Sometimes, it really wasn't worth the effort involved in trying to work out what adults were on about: I decided that this was one of those occasions.

Eventually, the long-awaited letter arrived and, to my amazement, I'd been selected. 'Your mother will be so proud of you,' the headmistress said, and when I got home from school that day, I burst through the back door shouting excitedly, 'They chose *me*! I'm going to the grammar school!'

It turned out that the headmistress had been wrong: my mother just grunted, raised her arm to push me out of her way, and said irritably, 'And who do you think is going to pay for your uniform?'

In the event, she didn't need to worry – although in fact I don't think it was actually concern about how she was going to find the money that prompted her complaint. Because my mother was a widow, she was given a grant to pay for the uniform and in the end she came out on top financially, as she so often did. A woman who went to the pub frequented by my mother and her boyfriend, Ernie Burns, offered her, for a very good price, a second-hand uniform that had been outgrown by her daughter, who already attended Rotherham Girls' High School. So my mother bought the uniform and pocketed the difference.

Despite being 'quids in' on the deal, she never really forgave me for getting into the grammar school. She wasn't proud of me at all, and she wasn't pleased that I'd been offered a great opportunity I'd never otherwise have had. On the contrary, the fact that I'd won a place at the school drove home, once and for all, the wedge that already existed between my mother and me and alienated us completely.

I haven't said much about Ernie Burns. I still find it difficult to talk about him, after all these years. My mother used to make us call him 'Uncle Ernie', but I still think of him as 'Ernie Burns'. Throughout my childhood, he was a constant, unwelcome presence in our lives – although not unwelcomed by my mother, of course. Their relationship – which was adulterous on his behalf – lasted for several years and I think she loved him. She certainly always put him first, however embarrassing that was for her children, and she always insisted he had to be invited to anything that involved the family, even when it was crystal clear that nobody else wanted him there.

When my brother Harry came home on leave during the war, he married his lovely girlfriend, Olive, who worked as a conductress on the buses, and of course Ernie Burns came to the wedding. My younger brother, Eddie, was still a little boy in short trousers and even though I was little more than a child myself, I remember feeling embarrassed because people stopped talking in mid-sentence and looked surprised when my mother reached over, took the flower from the buttonhole of Eddie's jacket and gave it to Ernie Burns. He wasn't a member of the family as far as we were aware and he'd only been invited to the wedding by Harry and Olive under duress. It didn't seem to matter to my mother that people were asking each other, 'Well, who is he? I thought she was a widow. Who's that man with her?' It mattered to us though – not that that would have made the slightest difference to either of them, even if they'd noticed our discomfort.

Whereas getting a place at the high school was the catalyst for breaking the already slight and tenuous bond that existed between my mother and me, it apparently prompted Ernie Burns to do the one nice thing he ever did for me in all the years he was involved in our lives – which was paradoxical, perhaps, in view of the fact that I didn't like him.

Shortly after I heard that I'd got a place at the high school, it was my birthday. My mother never bought us birthday presents, or even a card, so it didn't cross my mind that the leather satchel and wooden pencil case on the kitchen table were anything to do with me. When my mother waved her hand towards them and said petulantly, 'They're for you,' I didn't understand what she meant. I picked up the postcard that was propped up against the satchel, turned it over and read the words 'Happy Birthday', which were written on it in a hand that wasn't my mother's. She didn't tell me that the card and presents were from Ernie Burns, but I think they must have been. I suppose he felt I'd achieved something worthy of acknowledgement, even if my mother didn't, although that still didn't explain why someone who'd never bought me anything before – and who barely spoke to me – should do so now.

My mother and Ernie Burns still regularly went out

drinking together. For a while, their favourite pub was The Bridge, which was on an ancient bridge in Rotherham next to a small chapel where, legend has it, Mary Queen of Scots once prayed on her way to London. They'd go there almost every day and they became great friends with the landlord and his wife. Then something happened – as it always did – and suddenly they stopped going, some other pub became their favourite, and the whole process started again.

Oddly, considering he had a wife and family of his own, Ernie Burns always stayed the night at our house on Christmas Eve. Something else he and my mother always did was go away for a week every year to Redcar, for the racing. One year while they were away together, a woman approached Eddie when he was playing outside the house and asked him, 'Where's your mam?'

'I don't know,' Eddie told her, looking up briefly from where he was sitting beside another little boy at the edge of the pavement. 'She's not here. She's gone away.'

'Where's she gone?' the woman persisted. But Eddie didn't know.

Later, when he told me what had happened, I knew immediately that the woman was Ernie Burns' wife and that she'd been trying to find out what was going on. I'd never seen her or heard about any trouble between her and my mother, but I'm certain she knew, although she didn't come to our house again.

Except for Harry, who used to walk to school with me when I was very young, I didn't spend much time with my older brothers. They were all working and leading their own lives by the time I was five, and my mother never actively encouraged us to develop relationships amongst ourselves, except when it suited her purposes for some reason. So I don't know why she said to me one day during the war, 'You should write to Eric.' Eric was serving in the Navy as a deep-sea diver; we didn't know where he was, but when I sent him an airgraph, he answered it and we began to correspond regularly.

An airgraph was something that was introduced during the war to reduce the bulk and weight of all the letters that were being sent to sons, husbands and fathers who were fighting in almost every far-flung corner of the world. You'd write your letter as normal and then it would be photographed and sent – together with lots of others – as a negative on a roll of microfilm. When the film reached its destination, all the negatives would be printed on to photographic paper and delivered as airgraphs by the Army Postal Services. It only cost three (old) pence to send a letter that could have been going to the other side of the world, and I always looked forward to the ones Eric sent to me.

One way or another, the war changed the lives of countless people. Sixty million people died in the Second World War – two and a half per cent of the population of the world at that time – including an estimated twenty-five million military personnel. Many, many families – on all sides of the conflict – were left bereft; many parents lost sons and daughters who would never get married and have children of their own. So we were very lucky that all my brothers survived. Three of them got married during the war: Harry to Olive; John to Win, who was as gentle and as lovely as he was; and Bill to Renée. Unlike so many other people, our family was expanding. And, for me, it was about to expand even more.

My mother had married my father, Jack Manns, after the First World War and after he died in 1933, she didn't ever see or even talk about any of his relatives. I don't remember how I found out that I had cousins, on his side of the family, who were living near my school. When I did, I took it into my head one day to go and visit them. I didn't mention to my mother what I was planning to do. I'd long ago learned not to tell her things like that: if I did, she always told me I mustn't do it, whatever it was and however little it really mattered to her. So I just turned up on their doorstep one day after school, unannounced.

Luckily, my relatives were very pleased – as well as very surprised – to see me and I was invited into their house and made a great fuss of. One of the cousins, a boy, was learning to play the violin and his mother told me proudly, 'He's *very* clever. He'll play something for you.' The poor boy was embarrassed and very reluctant to show off his skills, particularly in front of a girl who, although apparently his cousin, he'd never met before. His mother wasn't taking no for an answer, however. She coerced and cajoled him until he picked up his bow – and played something that would have made the sound of a dozen cats screeching as they scraped their claws down a blackboard seem musical by comparison, even to my untutored ear.

It wasn't long after that when I discovered I had another relative, my father's sister, Beatty, who worked as a house-keeper in the town of Lytham St Annes, on the Lancashire coast. Auntie Beatty sent two lovely books for Eddie and me at Christmas and then she wrote a letter to my mother asking if, each of us accompanied by a friend, we could go and stay with her for a holiday. Fortunately, my mother was happy to get rid of us for a few days, and she agreed.

Eddie chose our sister Mabel's oldest son, Teddy, and I chose a friend from school called Margaret. We'd never had a holiday before and we were very excited. It turned out to be one of those things that are even better than you imagine they're going to be and we had a really lovely time. Auntie Beatty had booked us into a very nice boarding house where we were given *two* good cooked meals every day. In fact, we didn't see very much of her while we were there. She just gave us some pocket money and told us to go out and enjoy ourselves. I thought I'd died and gone to heaven!

When I was a child, it was glimpses into other lives and seeing other ways of living that were completely different from ours that made me realize it might be possible to choose an alternative to my mother's way of doing things. Even in my teens, it was hard for me to imagine being an adult, getting married and escaping from my mother's unremitting complaints and criticisms. People like Auntie Beatty, my Auntie Marion, my teachers and even the neighbours who were kind to me were role models for me in a way my mother never was. Drinking, gambling, effing and blinding whenever you spoke, having a long-term affair with someone else's husband, being indifferent to — at best — or openly disliking your children were all part of my mother's life; they didn't have to be part of mine.

I was fifteen when my mother came home from the pub one night, woke me up as she stumbled around the room I shared with her, and said, 'Jack Manns wasn't your father.' It's the sort of statement that drags you from half-asleep to wide awake in an instant.

It was a devastating announcement. You'd imagine anyone would deliver news like that in a careful, gentle way. But my mother never did anything carefully or gently and I doubt whether she even gave a moment's thought to how I'd feel about what she told me. I was still staring at her, open-mouthed in shocked astonishment, when she added, 'Your *real* father . . .' She stopped, expelled some trapped wind and, with the careful concentration of someone who's had a few too many glasses of Guinness, continued, 'Your *real* father is Uncle Ernie. And he's Eddie's father too.' Then she sat down heavily on the bed, swung her legs on to the mattress, fell into an awkward recumbent position, turned her back towards me and began to snore loudly.

I lay awake in the darkness for a long time with the words 'Ernie Burns is your father' going round and round in my head until they became sounds that no longer made any sense. Eventually I fell asleep too, and when I woke up the next morning, I wondered if it had all been a dream.

5

John Edward Manns – my mother's husband, the father of my four older brothers and the man who should have been *my* father and Eddie's – died after an operation to remove a tumour from his brain when he was just thirty-three years old, and I was two. Gradually, as the years passed, the few memories I'd had of him faded until they became like dim images in an old, sepia-coloured photograph. Discovering that he wasn't my father made me feel as though I'd lost him for a second time. Perhaps what was even more upsetting, however, was the knowledge of who my father *was*.

No allowance was ever made for emotional distress in our household. So I absorbed what my mother told me that night as best I could and did what we were always expected to do if anything bad happened: I got on with things, and she never spoke to me about it again.

I knew Eddie didn't like Ernie Burns any more than I did and I didn't tell him the true identity of the father we shared. Jack Manns had died before Eddie was born and when my brother was a little boy he sometimes used to say to me, 'It's not fair that you've seen my daddy and I haven't.' Somehow, telling him that wasn't the case after all didn't seem like the right thing to do.

In fact, Eddie didn't discover the truth until many years

later, when I think the news was even more traumatic for him than it had been for me. We were both in our fifties and Eddie was at a family wedding I hadn't been able to go to when our older sister, Mabel, told him – just like that, out of the blue. Mabel had always been a wonderful sister to both of us; she was the only person I knew really cared about me and loved me when I was a child, and I owe her more than I could ever have repaid. But as she got older – and she was already in her seventies at the time of the wedding – she could sometimes be a bit mean, although she was never spiteful in the way our mother had always been.

Eddie took the news very badly. I was talking to him on the phone late one night when he suddenly asked me, 'Is it true? Is Ernie Burns really our father?' I'd kept it a secret from him for all those years, but it would have been quite a different thing to have lied to him, and I told him yes, it was true. As soon as he'd put down the phone, Eddie went upstairs in his house and shaved off his moustache. Ernie Burns had had a moustache and while we were talking, the realization that he looked just like his biological father had hit Eddie like a thunderbolt from the sky.

It's difficult to describe how it feels to discover you aren't the person you thought you were. On the face of it, being told that a man you can't remember – or, in Eddie's case, never knew – didn't actually have any real connection with you shouldn't be such a terrible thing. It isn't even on the same scale as discovering – as some people do – that the father you love and who has always been a pivotal, fundamental part of your life from the day you were born isn't your father after all. It's still a traumatic experience though, and I think, all those years later, Eddie felt the same way I'd felt. For both of us, what was really hard to absorb and come to terms with was not so much that John Edward Manns wasn't our father as we'd always believed; it was discovering who our real father was, because none of us had ever liked Ernie Burns.

Not long after she'd told Eddie the truth, Mabel talked to me about the relationship my mother had had with 'Uncle Ernie' before I was born. Apparently, Ernie Burns worked with Jack Manns and was his friend. He often used to come to our house in the evenings and ask, 'Are you coming out for a drink, Jack?' Jack's answer was always the same: 'I don't earn enough money to go out drinking every night, Ernie. I'll have a glass of water from the tap if I'm thirsty. There's nothing to stop our Mabel going with you though, if she wants to.' (He meant my mother, of course, not my sister, who shared her name.)

The words were barely out of Jack's mouth before our mother was standing at the door, her coat in her hand and not even a backward glance. Her husband must have been either very trusting or very foolish. Whichever it was, he delivered my mother straight into the arms of the man who remained her lover for years and who cast a shadow over my entire childhood.

When I was twelve years old – before my mother's drunken nocturnal revelation – she was talking about Jack Manns one day when she suddenly said to me, 'He was so pleased to have a daughter after all those sons. Even when he was almost too ill to stand up, he used to carry you around.' Later, when I remembered what she'd said that day, I was glad to think that the poor man didn't know Eddie and I weren't his children.

Apart from buying the satchel and pencil box for me when I got a place at the high school, Ernie Burns never showed any sign that *he* knew the truth. He must have known though. How could he not? As I say, you only had to look at Eddie to see who his father was.

Ernie Burns wasn't a nice man, as my mother was later to discover; he certainly wasn't the man I'd have chosen – from a very long list of options – for a father. But things *are* what they *are* and, of course, I hadn't had any choice in the matter. In fact, no one ever asked my opinion or offered me an option about anything when I was a child, which is maybe at least part of the reason why I stuck so firmly and so determinedly to some of the choices I made later in my life.

My brother Eric was still away in the Mediterranean when, a few weeks before my fifteenth birthday, he sent me a letter asking me what I'd like as a present. It wasn't a question anyone had ever asked me before and when I wrote back telling him, 'I'd like a bike,' I was simply answering the question without any expectation of ever having one. When Eric's next letter arrived, I had to read parts of it twice, particularly the bit where he said, 'Tell my mother to take five pounds from my savings in the bank and give it you, so you can buy a second-hand bike.'

I think I was as happy about the fact that my brother *wanted* to buy me a bicycle as I was about the prospect of actually having one. I couldn't wait to tell my mother what

Eric had said. I thought she'd be pleased for me and as impressed by his kindness as I was. Looking back on it now, I can't imagine what made me think she'd have such an uncharacteristically maternal reaction.

'You greedy, selfish little . . .' She reached out her hand as she shouted at me and slapped the side of my head. Her anger took me completely by surprise and I burst into tears. 'How dare you?' she screamed, hitting me again. 'You're not having that money. You sit down this minute.' She pointed at the kitchen table. 'You sit there and write a letter to our Eric telling him you don't want the money to buy a bike for yourself; you'd rather he gave it to your mam and Eddie.'

'He asked me what I wanted,' I said, wiping the sleeve of my jumper across my tear-dampened cheeks. 'I didn't know he'd offer to buy it for me. But why, Mam? Why do I have to tell him I don't want a bicycle when I do? And why do I want him to give the money to you and Eddie?'

My mother cuffed me again and bellowed into my face, 'Because we deserve it and you don't, that's why.'

I was still sniffing and snivelling pathetically while I wrote a letter to Eric telling him – although not in so many words – that I didn't want the best present anyone had ever offered or was ever likely to offer to give me in my entire life. I never found out what he thought when he read my letter, but he did what I'd asked him to do and my mother took five pounds from his savings account to spend on herself and on my little brother, Eddie.

I couldn't understand at the time why my mother made me write that letter to Eric; it was years later when

I realized that the reason she reacted in the way she did was because she was jealous. My brother wanted to do something kind for me, and I think my mother truly believed *she* was the only one who deserved to be bought presents and made a fuss of. If there was anything left over after she'd bought what she wanted for herself, it should go to Eddie, her favourite child, rather than to me, her least favoured and a mere girl. I think she thought I might be at risk of getting a bit above myself, even to the extent of starting to believe I was 'better' in some way than she was, now that I was going to the high school – the first person in our family ever to have done so. She needn't have worried: one of her slaps accompanied by a cruel put-down was all that was required to remind me that I was stupid.

What no one except my mother knew at that time was that Eric was lucky to have had even five pounds in his savings account. He and Harry had been giving our mother a weekly allowance, as Eric had promised her he'd do when he joined the Navy, before anyone knew there was going to be a war. Every week, they were also sending her money to put in the bank for them so that they'd have something saved up when the fighting and post-war salvage operations were over and they came home.

Knowing my mother as I did, I can't imagine why anyone was surprised when Eric returned to Rotherham on leave a few months after the end of the war and discovered that very little of the extra money he and Harry had been sending had found its way into their accounts. I suppose Eric had thought it reasonable to believe that no one would steal from men who were many miles away from home fighting for king and country – least of all their own mother. Clearly, he didn't know our mother very well, or perhaps it was simply a case of absence making the heart grow fonder and the memory weaker.

Most of the money my brothers thought they'd been saving had been used by my mother to pay weekly instalments on furniture she'd bought from a catalogue to furnish the front room – the room that was rarely used, and that Eddie and I weren't even allowed to go into until we were old enough to be courting. She'd bought a carpet, a sideboard and a three-piece suite with curved wooden arms and with cushions covered in a plain brown fabric. We all thought it was very modern at the time; so much so, in fact, that when Mabel visited one day with a friend – which was another very rare occurrence, as we weren't encouraged to invite friends home with us – she asked if she could show her the room. Clearly, she was as proud of the new furniture as our mother was.

At least when they came home Eric and Harry could see exactly what their money had been spent on and they *were* allowed to sit on the three-piece suite with their girl-friends, although in winter they had to put their own shillings in the meter if they wanted to light the gas fire they'd also unwittingly bought with their savings.

Despite not having the money he'd expected to have when he came home, Eric told me, 'I *am* going to buy you a bike; you'll be able to ride it to school.' I think he was proud of me for getting into the high school; maybe that's why he wanted to do it, and, as luck would have it, I knew a girl who just happened to be selling her bicycle for five pounds, and Eric bought it for me.

I used to love cycling home from school, whizzing down the hills with the wind in my face and my heart in my mouth. When I was growing up, there was never money to buy anything that wasn't essential – certainly not for us children – and we didn't have many possessions. What I did have, thanks to Eric, was a bicycle that had been bought for me by my brother: I couldn't imagine anything better.

As I was flying through the streets on my way home from school one afternoon, I made the sharp turn from the hill into Eastwood Lane and when I squeezed the brakes on the handlebars, nothing happened. I knew I was going to take the corner far too fast, but there wasn't anything I could do about it. In spite of the high speed at which I was travelling, I managed to steer round the bend – and then I flew over the handlebars and smacked into a brick wall, missing the large, plate-glass window of a shop by just a couple of feet.

I don't have any memory of how I got to the hospital. Somehow I did, and as well as a huge, tender lump on my head and a deep cut on my face, it turned out that I had concussion. It might not sound like it, but I was lucky, because my injuries could have been a lot worse.

Eric was already back at sea by that time, and I don't know why my mother wrote to tell him what had happened. Perhaps she took spiteful pleasure from the fact that it was *his* gift to me that had been the means by which I'd hurt myself. It certainly wasn't because she felt sorry for me. With the exception of the day when I sat on her knee while we waited for the ambulance to arrive to take me and my brothers to hospital when we had diphtheria, she never showed any sign of sympathy for me or for anyone else. If it *was* spite that prompted her to write to Eric, she must have been irritated by the letter he sent in response, in which he asked, 'Why didn't you send me a telegram immediately to let me know what happened to our Sheila?'

Being at the high school meant I would be able, and expected, to stay on past the age of fourteen, which was the age at which all my older brothers had left school and started working. Unimpressed by the educational opportunities that had been opened up for me, my mother found me a job anyway: after all, I wasn't at school every hour of every day.

Another of the pubs my mother and Ernie Burns frequented was Duncan and Gilmour's. As well as being a 'good' customer, she also had a cleaning job there, and when I was fourteen she told me one day, 'I've got you a job in the evenings at the pub, doing the washing-up.'

'What about my homework, Mam?' I asked her. 'When will I do it if I'm working in the pub in the evenings?'

I don't think she even heard me; it wouldn't have made any difference if she had. So every day after school, I'd change out of my uniform, do as much homework as I had time for and then walk up the road to the pub, where I'd spend the evening washing glasses in the taproom.

Duncan and Gilmour's was at the bottom of a hill near a bus stop where dozens of men caught buses to the Park Gates Steelworks or the steelworks in Templeborough or Sheffield every day. In the summer, the pub doors on to the street would be opened, and sometimes when I was working at the sink, I'd see girls wearing my own high-school uniform getting off buses, laughing and talking, and I'd quickly duck down behind the bar so they wouldn't see me.

Night after night for months, I stood in that pub, breathing in the dense fog of cigarette smoke and the stench of stale beer, washing glasses until the skin on my hands was red and sore. The sound of my mother's loud, sometimes coarse laughter was clearly audible from where she was propping up the bar in the other room. She had reason to be cheerful because all the money I earned was paid directly to her; I didn't ever see even a penny piece of it.

I'd get home from the pub before Ernie Burns got back with my mother and I'd make myself scarce as soon as I heard them coming in. One night, I was still up when the back door flew open and they came into the house arguing. I stood up and was about to scurry upstairs when my mother said something to him – I didn't hear what it was – and as he turned to face her, he raised his arm as if to hit her.

I was across the room in four quick strides and, standing between them, I said, 'Don't you dare hit my mother!' He looked at me coldly for a moment, then dropped his arm and stormed out of the house.

As soon as the back door had slammed behind him, my mother turned on me and wailed, 'What did you do that for?' I suppose it was a good question, in view of the fact that she'd never have stood up for me against him, whatever the circumstances. I was hurt that she was angry with me when all I was trying to do was defend her, and I was even more upset when she told me the next morning, 'You'd better come home at dinnertime so that you can meet him when he gets off the bus and apologize to him.'

So later that day, when I should have been eating my lunch at school, I was waiting at a bus stop for Ernie Burns, feeling sick. When he jumped down off the bus, he was talking and laughing with a couple of other men and didn't seem to notice me. My heart was thudding and I could hear the echo of my heartbeat in my head as I took a few steps towards him and, swallowing hard, told him, 'I've come to say I'm sorry.'

For a split-second, his eyes flickered across my face; then he walked past me without a word, as though he hadn't heard or even recognized me. If he'd hoped to humiliate me, he'd succeeded: it was *awful*. I walked back to school with my cheeks burning and my vision blurred by tears of embarrassment and shame.

My mother and Ernie Burns liked betting on the horses. When you have very little money – and perhaps particularly if you work hard for what you do have, as my mother did – even the slimmest chance of winning some can brighten up your day. And they did win, sometimes, although never more than just enough to make them eternally optimistic and choose to overlook the fact that bookies *always* make more money out of gambling than their punters do.

There were some weeks when my mother would place bets on several days. In the mornings, she'd study all the horses and jockeys that were listed in the newspaper for every race; then, in the afternoons, she'd go up and down the hill to the house a few streets away where the bookie lived. Betting was illegal at that time and there were heavy fines for anyone caught taking punts. But the local bookie ran a very lucrative business, which enabled him to make regular payments to contacts who always made sure he knew in advance when the police were planning to raid his house.

My mother would bet three old pence, sixpence or, occasionally, as much as a shilling on a race, and she'd place bets for Ernie too, as well as for a couple of our neighbours, although their gambling was rather more sporadic. If the horse that Ernie or my mother had backed came in, they'd put their winnings on the next race, and so it would continue throughout the afternoon. Although her initial outlay was usually quite low, the money could add up over the course of a week to quite a significant amount.

Not far from our house there was a boys' club, which opened its doors to girls on Friday and Saturday nights. It was run by the church, so there was always a prayer and a short service to begin with, followed by table tennis and then – the moment most of us were waiting for – the record player would be brought out and the floor would be cleared for dancing.

It cost a shilling to get into the club, which my mother would give me to go once a week. It didn't seem too much to ask for out of the money I was earning – and never seeing – from working at the pub. Clearly, my mother didn't see it that way, and every single week when I asked her for it, she'd go on and on at me, telling me I didn't deserve it; I was lazy; I should be out working; did I think she was made of money? I longed for her, just once, to say to me, 'Yes, of course you can have a shilling. Here, take it and enjoy yourself.' It never happened, and I'd stand there in silence, looking at my feet and waiting for her to run out of reasons for not giving me the money or to lose interest in berating me, whichever occurred first. Enduring it always proved worthwhile in the end though, because I did *love* dancing.

It was at the boys' club that I met George Scholfield. I was fifteen and he was twenty. His home was in Halifax, where he and his sister had been brought up by their aunts after their mother died when George was very young. He'd been sent to Rotherham when he was conscripted to work as a Bevin Boy in one of its many coal mines.

During the war, coal couldn't be imported by sea to meet the increased demand for both industrial and domestic use, so more had to be produced in our own coal mines, which were already suffering from a shortage of manpower. In December 1943, the government came up with a solution: the Minister of Labour, Ernest Bevin, announced that one in ten men of call-up age would be selected by ballot to work in the mines – hence the name Bevin Boys. George was one of the conscript miners in a scheme that was continued until 1948, although he worked as a timekeeper rather than having to go underground.

George loved dancing as much as I did and it wasn't long before we were going steady.

6

As well as the boys' club, there were two dance halls in Rotherham and a drill hall, which had a swimming pool that was covered by a dance floor in the winter. Entry to the dance halls cost a shilling on weekdays and two shillings on Saturdays, which I could afford to pay if I'd earned some money doing knitting for someone or, during the school holidays, by working with my sister, Mabel.

There were a lot of farms around Hellaby, the village where Mabel and her husband Bill lived, and Mabel used to earn a bit of extra money by working on some of them, picking potatoes or peas, or doing whatever the farmers needed to be done at different times of the year. When I was fifteen, I started working alongside her in the holidays and although I still had to give most of the money I earned to my mother, she let me keep a bit of it – just enough to go dancing at the weekend with George.

Eddie and I had been lucky to spend weekends with Mabel and Bill when we were young. I was certainly grateful to Mabel for taking over the maternal role from my mother when she could; she became far more of a mother to me than ours had ever been. I really enjoyed working with Mabel on the farms, and we became good friends and grew closer as sisters. That was a good period in my young life, when I was going steady with George and I had Mabel to talk to.

Things were going well at school, too. When I'd started at the high school, I'd been anxious to keep up with all the new subjects I was learning and I'd worked hard. At seventeen, when I took the School Certificate Examination, I believed I had a chance of passing it. It wasn't a strong enough belief, mind you, to prevent my stomach churning as I opened the envelope containing the result.

One of the many things my mother used to say to me when she was annoyed with me – which was most of the time when I was a child – was 'You're neither use nor ornament.' I had no reason to believe it wasn't true – until I saw the word 'Passed' written on the piece of paper I pulled from the envelope with shaking hands. It was like hearing the faintest whisper of someone saying, 'You're not stupid after all.'

Knowing that I'd passed my School Certificate was even better than being told I'd been selected to go to the high school. *This* time, my mother couldn't fail to be impressed.

She was in the backyard and I ran down the passageway, waving the bit of paper above my head and shouting, 'I've passed! I've passed my School Certificate!' She didn't even look up. She just muttered, 'Oh, 'ave ya? I thought something must have happened, all the noise you're making.' Then she turned her back on me. She certainly had a way of putting me in my place.

I was determined not to let her see how hurt and

disappointed I was. I suppose I should have learned by that time that she simply wasn't interested and wasn't ever going to be interested in me or anything to do with me. But she knew how hard I'd worked and how important passing that exam was to me, and it would have been nice if, just once, she'd said she was happy for me.

What passing the exam meant in real terms was leaving school and getting a job, so that I could pay my mother for my board and lodging at home. Fortunately, there was plenty of work available in Rotherham in 1948. Of the 70,000 British civilians and close to 400,000 military personnel who'd been killed during the Second World War, most of the latter, at least, had been men of working age. So there were tens of thousands of gaps to be filled in the workforce, although at that time, and for some years to come, almost all the influential and managerial jobs were still held by men.

Within days of leaving school, I started working at Peck's, a large department store in Rotherham that sold everything from washing machines and furniture to shoes and clothes. There had been precious little of anything for anyone to buy during the war and people were tired of austerity. It was something the owners of Peck's were astutely aware of and credit became the mainstay of their business. People would buy things in the shop on credit and then a team of men would go round Rotherham every week to collect payments. It doesn't sound very innovative or remarkable today, when almost everyone buys on credit, but it was something new at the time. For the shop's customers, it meant being able to have immediately things they'd previously have had to save for months to buy, and for Peck's it provided a regular source of income from people who might otherwise not have been able to afford to shop there.

Making purchases on a shop account is a quick, simple, electronic process today. At that time, it involved the shop assistant phoning the office upstairs, where I worked, and giving me the customer's name and account details. Then I'd find the appropriate ledger and take it to one of the directors, who would either sanction or refuse the request, depending on the customer's credit record. Once a decision had been made, I'd phone downstairs and deliver the verdict to the shop assistant, who would pass it on to the happy or hapless shopper.

The work was neither interesting nor mind-stretching and it sometimes seemed as though the hands of the clock weren't moving at all. So when a girl who'd been in my class at school started working in the same office not long after I did, I was delighted. It didn't make the work any less boring, but at least I had someone to escape with at lunchtime every day. One day, unable to bear the thought of going back to work after lunch, we went to the pictures in town. The next morning, we told our boss we'd both been struck down by terrible headaches – and we got away with it! Maybe he knew that turning a blind eye to the occasional episode of truanting was the only way they'd manage to keep anyone employed in the monotonous jobs we were doing.

I was earning thirty shillings a week at Peck's. After I'd given my mother a pound, I had ten shillings to pay for bus fares to and from work, for going out at the weekends and for all my clothes. It wasn't much, even at that time, and I was beginning to feel restless. I wasn't happy living with my mother, who made me feel like an unwelcome stranger in my own home, and I decided the time had come to spread my wings and leave. The question was: where could I go? Leaving home wasn't simply a case of finding a flat to share with other girls, as it might be today: most young people – certainly all the ones I knew in Rotherham – lived at home with their parents until they got married. Then I had a bright idea: I'd join the Army! Without breathing a word to anyone about what I was planning to do, I sent off for the application forms.

It was late on a weekday morning and I was at work when someone told me that my brother John was down-stairs and wanted to talk to me. I ran down the stairs with my heart racing, trying not to think of all the things that might have happened that would have caused him to come now, in the middle of the day, to tell me about them.

It turned out that no catastrophe had befallen any member of the family. What had happened was that an envelope had arrived in the post at home for me and when my mother steamed it open (it wasn't something she felt the need to explain, so I can't do so either) it contained a warrant card sent – to *me* – by the Army so that I could go for a medical examination. As a result, John had been sent to fetch me home to answer my mother's questions. In fact, she didn't actually ask me any questions at all – at least, none that she waited for me to answer; she just shouted and swore at me and made it clear that joining the Army was not going to be an option for me after all.

It was a reaction that might have been understandable from a mother who feared for her daughter's safety and well-being. For my mother, it was all about the money I was giving her every week from my wages, and perhaps, too, about her simply wanting to stop me from doing anything I wanted to do.

I don't know why I was surprised to learn that my mother had steamed open an envelope addressed to me; she'd done the same thing a few months earlier, when I was still at school. On that occasion, it had been a letter from George. She didn't say she'd opened it, but I knew as soon as I saw the crinkled back of the envelope that she had.

So I didn't join the Army, and not long after I'd tried to apply, George Scholfield asked me to marry him. I didn't have to think for very long before I said 'yes': I was seventeen and a half, we'd been going out together for more than two years and I was very keen on George. Nothing changed for us immediately, except that suddenly I had a future to look forward to. Someone loved me enough to want to marry me, I was going to escape from my mother and I would have a home of my own. It all seemed too good to be true.

My pay at Peck's was poor, but it was the boredom that became too much to bear in the end. After I'd been working there for about nine months, I decided the time had come to move on and find something better. Once again, finding a job was easy, and I started work immediately at George Cohen Sons & Co., a metal-trading firm in the Sheffield suburb of Tinsley, just a short bus ride away from Eastwood Lane.

Everything about my new job was better than the old one, and I was delighted to find that another girl I'd been at school with – a girl called Jean – was working in the same office. I was very glad I'd made the move. If I hadn't, I wonder how different my life might have been.

One day, not long after I'd started work at Cohen's, George asked me to go with him to Halifax to visit his aunts for a weekend. We'd be staying at their house, so there was nothing improper about what he was suggesting, but when I asked my mother if I could go, she said 'no'. I couldn't understand why she was against the idea. I'd expected her to jump at the chance of getting me out of the way for a couple of days. I assume it was just a bit of spite, because she didn't like George and didn't want me to be happy, and I became determined that I *was* going to go.

I hadn't told her when the visit was due to take place and by the time the particular weekend came round, I knew she'd have forgotten all about it. And I was right, because when I told her I was going to stay with a friend, she just shrugged her shoulders in an eloquent expression of indifference, and I went to Halifax with George and stayed with his aunts, who were very nice to me.

When my mother didn't like someone, she was awful to them, and she could be so rude to George I'd just want to curl up and die from humiliation and embarrassment.

One of the reasons for her dislike of him was the fact that he didn't speak with a Yorkshire accent, which, to my mother, meant that he was – or, possibly even worse, he *thought* he was – 'posh'. The idea of someone 'getting above themselves' was anathema to my mother, which partly explains why she was so keen to cut me down to size when I got a place at the high school and again when I passed my School Certificate: she thought they were achievements that might prompt me to think I was better than she was.

One night, after we'd been out dancing and George had walked me home, as he always did, the house was empty and I invited him in for a cup of tea. We were sitting in the front room, on the brown settee, when he put his cup and saucer down on the floor, stared intently at the palm of his hand, he cleared his throat a few times, and then said, 'I don't think we're meant to be together, Sheila.'

At first I didn't understand and I smiled at him, in what must have looked like a very dim-witted way. The words were still rearranging themselves into a coherent sentence in my head when he coughed again and said, 'I'm sorry, Sheila. I want to break off our engagement.'

I could see that he was uncomfortable and embarrassed; all I was really aware of otherwise was feeling light-headed and a bit sick. I felt completely detached from him and from everything else in the room, as if I was watching through a window from outside. I think eventually I just said, 'I see. OK.' Then I slid the beautiful engagement ring George had given me off my finger and placed it carefully on the open palm of his hand.

I didn't cry until after he'd left the house, and then I sobbed as though my heart would break. I couldn't believe or understand what had happened. I hadn't noticed any change in our relationship at all, so what George had said had taken me completely and utterly by surprise. I was devastated.

When my mother came home from the pub I was still sobbing and, for once, instead of saying something nasty, she said, 'Oh well, you might be better off without him after all; you'll get over it,' which was as close to sympathetic as I'd ever known my mother to be.

I didn't have any friends I could confide in at that time. The only person I might have talked to about what had happened was my sister, Mabel; but I didn't. As well as being heartbroken and wretchedly miserable, I felt foolish and ashamed. I loved George and I'd thought he loved me, and now I suddenly realized that I wasn't good enough for him; it had been stupid of me to believe I was. I'd thought when he proposed to me that it was all too good to be true, and of course it was.

My mother was the sort of person who'd rather knock you down – and feel better herself by comparison – than build up your confidence with praise and encouragement. Even so, she wasn't entirely to blame for how I felt: I wasn't the only girl ever to have believed that if a man didn't want me, it must be *my* fault. Although I didn't really understand what had happened, there was one thing I was absolutely clear about: George had changed his mind about wanting to marry me because he'd realized my mother was right and I *was* neither use nor ornament. The chirpy little girl who'd been banished to a seat behind the blackboard on the first day of school because she couldn't contain her excitement and stop chattering had almost disappeared completely.

During the time my brothers Harry and Eric had been away in the war, I'd grown from a little girl into a tall, slim young woman with a mop of dark, fashionably curly hair. They'd both complimented me on the transformation and Eric had given my mother some money with the instruction to, 'Take our Sheila out and buy her something nice to wear. A whole outfit, mind.' Perhaps surprisingly, my mother had taken me to Peck's department store, where she did buy me an outfit, although she couldn't resist the temptation to buy it on credit and pocket the cash Eric had given her.

I'd always been in awe of Eric, both because he was my older brother and because of his innate air of authority, and I'd been secretly elated when he and Harry had said nice things about me. But when George jilted me, I felt embarrassed by my naivety: Eric and Harry were my brothers; they didn't see me as other boys saw me, and their comments had been based purely on the fact that, while they were away, I'd grown from gawky little sister to young woman. I was stupid to have believed anything else.

When I bumped into George many years later, he told me he'd broken off our engagement because of the way my mother had been. I wish I'd known that at the time. Although it probably wouldn't have changed anything between George and me, at least I might not have blamed myself as much as I did. What happened next, however, was nobody's fault but my own.

There were a lot of men working at George Cohen's and a lot of banter – it was in the days before anyone had even thought of banning sexist comments from the workplace. There was also the inevitable office gossip – which can never be legislated against – and one day the girls were talking about a man who'd asked another girl out. When the girl from my school who I'd become friends with said she thought the man was married, someone else disagreed. As I'd only ever exchanged a couple of words with him in passing, I didn't take much notice of what they were saying.

A few days later, though, the man they'd been talking about stopped and spoke to me in the corridor. We talked briefly about inconsequential things and then he asked me if I'd like to go to the cinema with him. I was eighteen and he was in his early thirties, quite attractive and very pleasant. After being jilted by the man I was in love with, I firmly believed that no man would ever be interested in me again. So I was flattered by his attention. I hadn't told anyone that George had jilted me, of course – I was far too ashamed. But people talk, and everyone knows someone who knows someone you know, so it was possible it wasn't the secret I believed it to be. I did wonder later if the invitation to go to the cinema had been prompted by the knowledge that I was suffering from a broken heart and would therefore be likely to respond positively to any interest shown in me by another man.

After we'd been to the cinema together, we went to a café, where we ate beans on toast and drank cups of tea. I'd never even set foot in a café before that day and, as ridiculous as it sounds now, I'd never eaten food like that.

We had a few more dates after the first one, although not on any regular basis. I didn't know whether he was seeing other girls – I don't think I even thought about it. I did know, however, that he was married, although separated and living apart from his wife. When we went out together, he talked about all sorts of things, including the places he'd been and his experiences in the RAF during the war. To a girl from Rotherham who'd never ventured further afield than Sheffield, it felt as though I was being given a glimpse of a sophisticated world that was completely different from the only world I'd ever known; the whole experience was a revelation to me. I was beguiled by him and it was the easiest thing in the world to get caught up in the moment. I was naive and gullible, and on the cold, damp November night when he asked me to go with him to the flat he rented above a shop in Sheffield, I didn't even stop to think.

7

At his flat, he gave me a drink, showed me photographs that had been taken of him in his RAF uniform and told me how pretty I was and how much he enjoyed my company. I wondered later if he'd planned what happened that night, although it never even occurred to me at the time that I might be being used. My greatest fear was to be discarded again, as George had discarded me. I suppose that's why I allowed my head to be turned by his attention and a few words of flattery, and why I did what he wanted me to do.

I was still seeing him occasionally when I missed my period. Despite being naive about the act of sex itself, I did have some knowledge of biology and I knew immediately that I was pregnant. Being pregnant and unmarried in 1950 was something you wouldn't wish on your worst enemy. If people did something that went against the social norm in those days, no one sympathized or tried to understand. It was simple: there were 'nice' girls and there were the other sort, who brought shame on themselves and on their families and who were 'no better than they ought to be'. And that was the sort of girl I'd now become.

The doctor confirmed what I already knew and when I told 'the father', he looked at me for a moment with a cold expression on his face; then sighed and said, 'Oh hell!'

'Why didn't you *do* something?' I asked him plaintively. 'Why didn't you take some precaution so that it couldn't happen? I just assumed you'd done that.'

There was no contraceptive pill in 1950. Contraception was something men took care of – as they took care of so many things at the time – although not all men, it seemed.

He shrugged his shoulders and, with a nasty, humourless laugh, said, 'Well, that would be a bit like going to bed with your socks on, wouldn't it?'

I didn't see the similarity at all. What I did see, however, with sudden, brilliant clarity, was how shallow he really was. I didn't know how I could have failed to notice it before.

Telling him was just the first of the many hurdles that faced me. The next one was to find the courage to tell my mother. I had no idea what I was going to say to her; I kept putting it off until, one day, I just blurted out, 'I'm pregnant.'

Few of my mother's sentences managed to stagger from capital letter to full stop without a liberal sprinkling of swear words, and she reached new heights of profanity that day. This time though, as she ranted and raved at me and told me how stupid I was, I would have been hard pressed to find any reason to argue with her.

Telling my mother I was pregnant was one of the hardest things I'd ever had to do, but I knew that the third hurdle was going to be the most difficult one of all. I dreaded having to tell my brother Eric. Of all my brothers, he was the one who'd been kindest to me. He really seemed to love me and the pride he clearly had in me was

81

the only source of the little pride I had in myself. I felt sick to the pit of my stomach when I thought about telling him. So I suppose I should have been grateful to my mother for doing it herself.

I hadn't told her who the 'culprit' was — just that he was someone at work — and I didn't tell Eric either. In fact, when Eric erupted into rage, I didn't say anything to him at all. What was even harder to bear than his anger, however, and what hurt more than anything else was his obvious disgust with me. When he eventually stopped shouting at me, he didn't speak to me again until the next day, when he told me coldly, 'I've made an appointment to see a solicitor.' Those were the only words he addressed to me until I met him after work outside a solicitor's office in town.

The reason for the appointment was for Eric to find out what legal action could be taken against the unscrupulous cad who'd taken advantage of his sister. My brother was deeply disappointed in me and repulsed by what I'd done, and he was absolutely enraged to think that the, as yet unidentified, Lothario who'd impregnated me could simply walk away scot-free. So he was incensed when the solicitor told him there was no recourse in the law to make the blackguard pay.

While Eric and the solicitor talked to each other as if I wasn't there, I sat with my head bowed and my hands tightly clasped on my lap, wishing that the floor would open and swallow me up. It was a dreadful, terrible experience and it made me feel far worse about what had happened than anything else had done.

When we left the solicitor's office, Eric turned his back on me without a word and strode away down the street. By the time I got home, he'd already poured himself a glass of whisky and was pacing up and down the kitchen as he told my mother what the solicitor had said. All the time, he was taking sips from the glass in his hand and when he finally turned his attention to where I was sitting, meek and wordless in a chair beside the kitchen table, he'd refilled it twice and his cheeks were flushed.

The next few minutes seemed like an eternity as he ranted and raved at me, pausing occasionally to jab his finger a few inches from my face to emphasize his disgust and disappointment in me. Then he stopped pacing, stood directly in front of me and shouted, 'I wash my hands of you.'

He must have tightened his fingers around the glass as he released his last outburst of anger, and it shattered into pieces, cutting his hand and sending trickles of blood along the inner surface of his wrist. I put my own hands on the table to push myself up and out of the chair I was sitting in so that I could help him, but he turned away from me, shouting as he did so, 'Get out of my sight. I want nothing more to do with you.'

After the war had ended, Eric had still had three of the twelve years he'd signed up for to serve in the Navy. While at home, he'd become very ill with meningitis and spent some time in hospital. It was touch and go for a while, and he was lucky to recover. By the time he did, he'd decided he didn't want to go back to sea. There was a shortage of coal miners after the war, and when Eric found out that he could commute his last three years in the Navy to work in the recently nationalized coal industry, he'd jumped at the chance.

He knew what he was letting himself in for – wanting to escape from the mines had been the reason he'd joined the Navy in the first place – but he must have felt at the time that it was the lesser of two evils. In fact, he ended up working in an office rather than going down the pit itself and the decision he'd made changed the course of his life when he got involved with the miners' trade union and with local politics, worked for a degree at Sheffield University in his spare time and was subsequently elected as a local councillor.

It took a lot of hard work and determination for Eric to make what he did of his life. Some of that determination was apparent in the fact that, true to his word, after he'd taken me to the solicitor that day and then shouted at me at home in the kitchen, he never willingly spoke to me for the next sixteen years. He was a man of strong principles and opinions and I knew he felt that I'd betrayed the trust he'd had in me. I understood that he'd been proud of his little sister and that what I'd done had hurt him deeply. What I didn't ever understand, though, was why he couldn't find it in his heart to forgive me.

After cutting his hand on his whisky glass on that horrible day, Eric stormed out of the house, slamming the back door behind him, and it was left to my mother to decide what to do with me. Apparently, she already had a plan.

After adding hot coals to the grate underneath the copper in the kitchen, she went down into the cellar and, a few seconds later, I heard the familiar clunking sound as she carried the metal bath up the steps. I watched in silence as she put the bathtub on the floor in front of the fire and began to fill it with steaming hot water from the copper. When it was a little more than half full, she told me to get in, handed me a quarter bottle of gin and said, 'Drink that, all of it; then go to bed.' So that's what I did.

I don't remember how I got from the kitchen to the bedroom. I was crying when I climbed into the bath and the next thing I was aware of was leaning over the side of the bed vomiting violently. I could hear a loud, persistent hammering sound, which seemed to be coming from inside my head, and I can remember thinking anxiously how furious my mother was going to be when she discovered what I'd done to the rug. And then I must have fallen asleep.

I don't know how much later it was when I opened my eyes just enough to make out shapes and patches of light through my eyelashes. I thought I saw my mother kneeling on the floor by the bed with a bucket of water, mopping up the foul-smelling mess.

When I woke up the next morning, the thudding in my head had become a dull, throbbing pain and my eyelids ached when I tried to open my eyes. It was my mother's only attempt to abort the baby I was carrying. After that night, she restricted her involvement in my pregnancy to terse questions about what I was going to do. 'There's only one thing I *can* do,' I said eventually. 'I'll have the baby and then I'll have it adopted.'

I don't know whether magazines still have 'agony aunts' today. I expect they do, although I imagine that the problems they're presented with and the advice they offer are very different from what they used to say in the 1940s and 1950s. The letter I wrote was to *Woman* magazine. I think the walls of the entire house could have been papered with all the bits of notepaper I screwed up and discarded as I attempted to find the right words to explain that I was single and pregnant, that my mother was adamant I couldn't keep the baby and it would have to be adopted, that I'd heard there were places where girls in my situation could go to have their babies, and that that's what I wanted to do; so could they please help me to find somewhere, hidden away from my friends, family and neighbours, where I could have the baby?

Someone at the magazine responded with a letter giving details of an organization run by the Church of England. I rang the phone number, which was for an office in Sheffield, and spoke to a woman with a brisk, businesslike voice who made an appointment for me to go there for an interview after work one day during the following week.

I was just three months' pregnant and I doubt whether anyone who saw me on the bus on my way to Sheffield would have guessed my shameful secret. It felt to me, though, as if everyone who caught my eye could tell I was

86

hiding something, and I barely turned my head away from the window.

The woman who sat opposite me across the wooden desk in the drab, sparsely furnished room in a dilapidated Victorian house in Sheffield told me, 'The home you'll be going to is in Huddersfield. You'll go there six weeks before your due date and remain for six weeks after the birth. When the baby's born, you'll take care of it yourself until it's adopted.'

She didn't give me any details of what she called 'the adoption process' or tell me anything about how the people who would become the parents of my child would be selected. And I didn't ask. I knew what I'd done was 'wrong', and I didn't expect sympathy or kindness from anyone, or to be offered a choice about anything. I was just thankful there was somewhere I could go to have the baby before I went home again and tried to pretend that none of it had ever happened.

It was unusual at that time for families to offer support and assistance of any kind to girls like me, and as the state didn't provide a safety net, financial or otherwise, as it does now, it was virtually impossible for unmarried girls to keep their babies and care for them themselves. Consequently, many girls were sent away to distant towns to give birth in unmarried-mother-and-baby homes like the one I was going to go to, and then their babies were adopted. There was no question of having a choice. You knew you were lucky that anyone was willing to help you at all.

I accepted without question the arrangements that

would be made for me, and my mother must have been satisfied with them. After I'd told her what was going to happen, she didn't mention it again. In fact, she played no part in anything related to my pregnancy. Her sole concerns were that the birth should not cause her any trouble or inconvenience and that no one should know I had brought such terrible shame on my family by getting myself pregnant – which was pretty rich coming from someone who'd been having an affair with a married man for years, had had several miscarriages, both natural and otherwise, and, having given birth to two children fathered by her lover, wrote her husband's name on their birth certificates without a second thought.

When I saw 'the Lothario' to tell him what I was going to do, it was clear that he'd already dissociated himself completely from what had happened and had no further interest in me. I was on my own: that was how things were going to be from now on, until after the birth of my child, at least. In fact, I didn't think of the baby that was growing inside me as 'my child'. I knew the only way I was going to be able to get through the ordeal that lay ahead was by remaining detached and not allowing myself to think about it as a human being at all.

The only other person outside my immediate family who knew I was pregnant was my friend Jean, the girl I had become friends with at George Cohen's. And she was absolutely the only person to whom I revealed the identity of the father. I told her because I had to share the secret with someone, and she'd been very sympathetic – to my face. Unfortunately, however, while she'd been encouraging me to confide in her, she'd also been spreading the news around the office.

It was just a few days after I'd been to Sheffield when the manager at work stopped me as I was walking down the corridor and said, 'Ah, Sheila. I'd like a word with you.' Opening the door of an empty office, he smiled a very small smile and asked, 'Shall we go in here and have a quick chat?'

When we were inside the room and he'd closed the door behind us, he looked at me with an expression I couldn't read and said, 'Now, Sheila.' He cleared his throat. 'I'm sorry to embarrass you like this, but I've heard something about you and I need to know if it's true.'

My heart sank from my chest to my feet like a lift with a cut cable, and I had to wait until it hit the ground before I was able to whisper, 'Yes, it's true.' Crossing my arms in a subconscious gesture of self-protection, I waited for the words I knew were coming.

'Well.' The manager coughed, then raised his right hand and patted my shoulder awkwardly. 'Well,' he said again. 'I just wanted you to know that we'll do whatever we can to help you. You only have to ask.' I was still wondering if I'd really understood what he'd said when he opened the door, smiled at me briefly, then stepped out into the corridor and walked away. For a few seconds I continued to stand in the empty room, listening to the sound of his receding footsteps and trying to make sense of what had just happened and of the fact that I wasn't going to be sacked, as I'd fully expected to be.

The company did sack 'the culprit', however, which I

think was quite an unusual step to have taken at a time when, of the two of us, the sternly wagging finger of society's disapproval would have been reserved almost exclusively for me.

Since becoming employed as an office clerk at George Cohen Sons & Co., I'd been going almost every day at lunchtime to the deserted typing pool to teach myself to type. So I was delighted when, a few days after my talk with the manager, I was told that I was being sent to join the other typists who worked there. It was a delight that was short-lived, however.

I knew that my 'friend' Jean had been the one who'd spread the story: she was the only person who knew the identity of the man I'd slept with. But I didn't have enough self-confidence to blame her, even to myself, for what she'd done. Jean and another, older, woman did the filing for the typing pool, and between them they made my life a misery. After putting up with their whispered, huddled conversations, which ended abruptly whenever I came into the room, for as long as I could bear it, I decided to look for a job elsewhere, where no one knew my secret.

Again, it didn't take me long to find work – this time as a typist for the recently created National Assistance Board, which later became absorbed into the Department of Health and Social Security. I liked the people I worked with, and if, as the weeks passed, they noticed I was putting on weight in a rather odd way, no one said anything, or treated me any differently because of it. In fact, I was fortunate in that I didn't develop a distinct bump, so

I was able to convince myself – as my mother had clearly done – that no one guessed I was pregnant.

When I told my doctor about the arrangements that had been made for me to go to Huddersfield six weeks before my due date, I confided in him that I was very worried about losing my job. I wanted to ask the company to keep it open so I could return to it when the whole sorry business was over and I was trying to unravel the tangled threads of my life. To do that, however, meant having to come up with some explanation as to why I was going away for three months.

'Oh, that's all right,' the doctor said, reaching across his leather-topped desk and pulling a pad of paper towards him. 'I'll write a note to say you can't work because you've got a growth in your stomach.'

My surprise must have shown on my face, because he smiled at me and lifted his shoulders in a gesture of exaggerated mock indignation. 'What?' he asked. 'Well, it's true, isn't it?'

As result of the note he wrote, I was able to take sick leave instead of having to quit my job for no reason I could explain to anyone.

On the morning of the day I'd hoped would never come, I packed a small suitcase and left the house on Eastwood Lane to walk to the bus stop and catch a bus to Sheffield, from where I'd get another to Huddersfield. I was setting out on a journey I didn't want to make, to go to a town I didn't want to go to, where I'd do something I wished I didn't have to do. But things *are* what they *are*, and it was a journey I knew I had to make.

8

When I arrived at the large, double-bay-fronted Victorian house in Huddersfield, I paused for a moment on the pavement outside and put down my suitcase while I checked the house number against the address written on the damp, crumpled piece of paper in my pocket. Then I took a very deep breath, picked up my suitcase, opened the little wooden gate and walked the short distance down the path to the black-painted front door.

When I leaned forward to ring the highly polished brass bell, the thought flashed through my mind to turn and run before it was too late. Then, as the door was opened by a middle-aged woman with an unsmiling expression that seemed to be just one small muscle-twitch away from open disapproval, I almost imagined I could hear the sound of a door closing behind me and I remembered that I had nowhere to run to.

'You'll be Sheila Manns.' It was a statement of fact spoken in a voice that, although not friendly, wasn't unkind, by a woman who was clearly not accustomed to being contradicted. 'Come in.'

During the previous few weeks, since the arrangements had been made for me to go to the unmarried-mother-and-baby home in Huddersfield, I'd avoided thinking about what it might be like. Now, though, as I stepped through the front door on to the highly polished wooden floor of the hallway, the realization struck me that I'd come to a place where everyone would know I was pregnant and where anyone who wasn't in the same situation as I was would be likely to censure or even openly criticize me. I could feel myself blushing.

Inside the house, the woman had disappeared through an open doorway on the left of the front door, leaving me standing in the hallway, clutching my suitcase so tightly that the muscles in my arm began to ache. She appeared again after a couple of seconds and said impatiently, 'Don't just stand there, girl. Come in.'

The room I followed her into was clearly being used as an office and as she sat down behind a heavy oak desk, she waved her hand towards a wooden chair on the near side of it and said, 'Sit. Sit down.' Then she pulled a small metal box across the desk towards her, selected a key from several that hung on a chain at her waist and, as she opened the box, told me, 'I need your money-order book. You'll be given a small allowance each week and the rest will be put towards the cost of your food and board while you're here. There are rules, of course, which will be explained to you and to which you will adhere at all times. You will not leave the house until after the baby has been born, when you will do so only with permission and accompanied. Do you understand?'

A lump had formed in my throat while she was talking, and I was still trying to swallow it when she asked again, this time with exaggeratedly careful enunciation, 'Do you understand?' I lowered my eyes and nodded.

'Now, you need to sign this form.' Her tone was brisk again as she pushed it across the table towards me and handed me a pen. 'Doing so confirms that you want your baby to be adopted.'

After I'd signed my name, I followed her up the wide staircase, one hand holding my little suitcase, the other clasping the gleaming wooden handrail. At the top of the stairs, she crossed the landing, opened a door into a large bedroom and said, 'This is your room. You can put your clothes in here.' She bent down and pulled open the bottom drawer of a heavy oak chest. 'I'll leave you to unpack your bag. Lunch will be in twenty minutes. The dining room's on the left at the bottom of the stairs. It's the door opposite the office.'

When she'd gone, I stood in the bedroom, clutching my suitcase and wishing I was almost anywhere else on earth. Now, more than at any other time in my life, I didn't want to be alone in unfamiliar surroundings in a house full of strangers; but I had no choice. My mother had made it clear I couldn't stay at home to have the baby and I'd had no sympathy or practical support from any member of my family. Although Eric had been the most vociferous in his condemnation of me, all my older brothers had been unanimous in their disgust at what I'd done. However much I dreaded the weeks that stretched ahead, I knew I was lucky to have somewhere to stay at all.

Eventually, I put my suitcase down on the wooden floor, walked over to the large sash windows that almost filled the wall opposite the door, and lifted the corner of one of the white net curtains that covered them. The bedroom was at the front of the house and the windows looked out on to a suburban road and a small garden divided into two patches of lawn by the path I'd walked up when I arrived.

After a moment, I let the curtain drop and turned to examine the bedroom. It was a large room, spotlessly clean, with four beds, although there was little sign that anyone actually slept in them. Three of the beds were very neatly made up and on the fourth – which I assumed was mine – there was a pile of precisely folded grey woollen blankets, stiff white sheets and a worn, lumpy pillow, on top of which was a leather-bound Bible. Apart from the chest of drawers and a washbasin in one corner of the room, the only other furniture was a small wooden chair beside each bed.

It didn't take me long to transfer my few meagre items of clothing from the suitcase into the drawer, and I was in the process of making up the bed when the door of the room burst open. The small, dark-haired girl who stood in the doorway looked younger than my little brother Eddie. She narrowed her eyes and regarded me appraisingly for a moment, and then she smiled and said, 'I'm Mavis. I've been sent to tell you to come down for lunch.' Then she turned and I could hear the loud thud of her footsteps as she ran down the stairs. I walked out of the room, closing the door behind me, and followed her.

In the dining room, there were already seven girls seated around the table and they all turned to look at me as I stepped through the door. The woman who'd let me in when I arrived at the house was there too, as well as another woman, who nodded at me briefly before saying, apparently to no one in particular, 'This is Sheila.' None of the girls said anything and none of them looked at me again while we ate our meal in almost uninterrupted silence.

I found out later that some of the other girls staying in the house had already had their babies, and although they seemed to be quite friendly with each other, they rarely spoke to me. The one thing we all had in common was the one thing none of us wanted to talk about, and the two women who ran the home did nothing to discourage our disinclination to get to know each other. In fact, they rarely spoke to us either, except to issue instructions.

Both women were in their forties, or perhaps early fifties, and wore almost identical dark-coloured, calf-length skirts. I never saw either of them smile. We certainly owed them a debt of gratitude for taking us in, but they didn't hide the fact that, in their eyes, we were sinners – as we were in the eyes of most other people too. It was clear that they were simply there to do a job, which was to provide us with regular meals and a roof over our heads and make sure we didn't get any opportunity to repeat the sinful error for which we were currently paying the price. They had no empathy for us at all, and we didn't expect them to. Although I wouldn't have chosen to be there, I did appreciate the fact that the women and the church organization for which they worked had offered me a refuge my own mother hadn't been prepared to give me. A home for unmarried mothers wasn't a happy or a comfortable place to be in 1950, but I believed – as society did at that time – that discomfort was no less than I deserved.

It turned out that Mavis – the girl who'd come to the bedroom to tell me lunch was ready – didn't work at the home, as I'd imagined she did because she looked so young. She was one of my roommates. The others were a girl called Annie, who, like Mavis, didn't show any visible signs of being pregnant, and another called Flo.

On my first night at the home, I lay on my back in bed, on a hard, lumpy mattress between two cold starched sheets, with my eyes wide open and a lump in my throat that refused to be swallowed, and listened while Mavis told me her story.

'I knew I'd been putting on weight,' she said. Then she laughed the way people do when they know you won't believe what they're going to say next. 'And then I woke up one morning feeling sick. I didn't think anything of it at the time. Then it happened again the next morning and the morning after that and me mam took me to see the doctor.'

After examining Mavis, the doctor had asked her mother, 'You do know that your daughter's pregnant, don't you?' Mavis's mother didn't know it, of course, any more than Mavis did. In fact, it was probably the last explanation she'd have thought of, because Mavis was just twelve years old.

Even today, when children seem to remain children for a much shorter time than they did sixty years ago, twelve is extremely young to be pregnant. In 1950, it was virtually unheard of, certainly as far as I was aware. So I was shocked when Mavis told me her age; and I was rendered completely speechless when she said that her own father was the father of her unborn child.

At first I didn't understand what she meant. And then she told me, almost carelessly, about how her father used to sneak into her room at night to wake her up when she was asleep and rape her.

The gasp escaped from my open mouth before I could stop it. I was only thankful it was dark, so no one could see the horror I knew was written all over my face.

'The problem was . . .' Mavis paused as if she was about to reveal the *first* problem of her story so far. 'Because I was getting big, he was starting on my little sister.' She made it sound like something mundane and unremarkable, rather than the incestuous rape of a little girl by her own father – although I don't know what sort of voice one *would* use to describe something so unimaginably awful.

'When Dad was arrested,' she continued, 'I had to go to court and they asked me all these questions.'

'That must have been very hard for you,' I said at last, in a cracked, high-pitched voice that didn't sound like mine.

'Yeah, well, he went to prison for it, did my dad,' Mavis said, and then, apparently oblivious to the effect her words were having on me, she described in detail what had happened during the court hearing and how she'd ended up coming to Huddersfield, to the home for unmarried mothers and their babies.

I couldn't help wondering what she must think about

when she lay in bed in the darkness, or during the daytime when she was doing chores around the home and waiting for the birth of the child that would be whisked away immediately, without her ever even seeing it. Because of the circumstances of its conception, Mavis's baby would be taken as soon as it was born to a Dr Barnardo's home, where he or she would remain, without ever being given the chance to be adopted, until old enough to live independently. The future didn't look good for either of them, and I felt desperately sorry for Mavis and for her unborn child.

In those days, no one ever talked about what went on behind closed doors, and I'd had no idea that the sort of things Mavis told me about that night ever occurred anywhere, to anyone. Being pregnant because one had had sex before marriage *as an adult* was considered to be deeply shameful, so what also surprised me about Mavis's revelations was why anyone would *want* to talk about things like that, particularly to a complete stranger. Looking back on it now, I wonder if perhaps the fact that Mavis *didn't* know anything about me other than that I was pregnant and wasn't married was what made her feel able to tell me the things she told me that night.

I'd been at the home for a couple of days and was still in a state of shock following Mavis's revelations when Annie, one of the other girls who shared our bedroom, told me an equally shocking story. Annie was fourteen and the father of the child she was carrying was her brother. I didn't have a father – at least, not a father who was acknowledged as such or who lived with me – but I did have brothers, and I couldn't even begin to imagine how such a terrible thing could ever happen.

Society has changed radically in many ways since 1950. It could be argued that *some* of the things that are discussed so openly and in such detail today might be better left unsaid. For example, open almost any magazine or newspaper and it's difficult to avoid learning things you'd far rather not know about the private lives of 'celebrities' you've barely even heard of. But at least people are now more aware of the appalling treatment many children suffer at the hands of adults who should be taking care of them; and that awareness might one day lead to a remedy.

The willingness to discuss things openly also means that girls and women are no longer forced by an intolerant, unforgiving society to give up their children at birth. There's no real stigma attached to being unmarried and pregnant today: it's commonplace and often the result of choice; whereas in 1950 it was a cardinal, unforgivable sin and girls in my position went to great lengths to hide the shameful truth from other people, and so did their families.

All these years later, I still sometimes think about Mavis and Annie and wonder what became of them and their babies. I hope they got the help they needed and that they and the children they never knew went on to lead happy lives.

At the time, it felt as though I'd stepped into another world I hadn't even known existed and that, although I felt sorry for Mavis and Annie, I wished I hadn't become part of.

Probably in contrast to the normal lives of all the girls staying at the home when I was there, the 'two Misses' made sure that everything took place in an orderly, organized manner. Every day started early, when one of the women knocked sharply on the door of the bedroom and told us to get up. A few minutes later, I'd walk down the stairs dressed in one of the only two dresses I owned – both of which had elastic in their waists to accommodate my now rapidly enlarging bump. I'd sit in the kitchen at the back of the house with the other girls while we quickly drank our cups of tea and ate a slice of bread. Then we'd file out of the kitchen and into the room next to the dining room, which had been converted into a small chapel.

The purpose of the tea and slice of bread was to stop us fainting during the short service that consisted of a couple of mumbled prayers and the unenthusiastically tuneless singing of a hymn. Afterwards, we'd go back into the kitchen to eat a proper breakfast before making a start on whatever chores had been allocated to us for that particular day.

The girls who'd already given birth didn't take part in the daily cleaning of the house. Their mornings were occupied feeding their babies, changing and washing nappies, and all the other tasks involved in taking care of a newborn baby – about which I knew next to nothing.

By the end of the morning of the first full day I was at the home, I'd realized why everything in the house shone and why you could have run your finger along any surface at any height in any room without finding even the slightest trace of dust or dirt. We were 'the help' who did all the work, and the two women were our exacting taskmasters.

On my first day, I was given the job of cleaning and polishing the already gleaming, apparently pristine hall floor. It was a job that required doing battle with the 'bumper'. The bumper was a Heath-Robinson-inspired contraption consisting of a long pole at the end of which was a heavy, oblong piece of wood and metal and a wad of soft material. Every single inch of the floor had to be cleaned with this instrument of torture until the wood was buffed to the supernatural state of cleanliness required to satisfy the high standards set by our two eagle-eyed custodians. It was a horrible job, so I was thankful when I discovered that every few days we alternated between tasks.

There was a method for doing each job that we were supposed to follow to the letter, and woe betide anyone who tried to cut corners: they never did it twice. Every day, every inch of the house had to be mopped, polished and dusted; the brass letterbox, knob and knocker on the front door had to be buffed and cleaned until they shone; and the front steps had to be scrubbed before applying donkey stone to their edges. They were jobs that the skivvy maid in the kitchen would have done when the house was first built as a family home, and probably up until the end of the First World War. Now, we did them.

We weren't supposed to feel that we were 'at home' in any way, which meant that we weren't even allowed, for example, to go into the kitchen to make ourselves a cup of tea. All our meals were cooked by the two women and eaten in the dining room. Some of the girls clearly had mothers who were better cooks than mine was, and they often moaned and complained about what was served to us. It was plain, simple food, which was more than adequate for our needs, and no one insisted we had to eat what was put in front of us; if you didn't eat it, you went hungry.

Our main meal was at lunchtime, and one day it was marrow stuffed with minced beef and onions. My mother wasn't an adventurous cook – which was probably a good thing, considering the torture she inflicted on even the simplest of ingredients – and I'd never even seen a marrow before. The only vegetables we ever ate at home were dried peas that had been steeped for hours in water, soggy cabbage that was only recognizable because of its overpowering odour, and, very occasionally, cauliflower. So although the other girls pulled faces and complained that the smell of the mince and onions was making them feel sick, stuffed marrow seemed very exotic to me, and I thought it tasted delicious.

I don't think it was with any expectation of a positive response that one of the women asked, 'Does anyone want a second helping?' And every head turned towards me when I lifted my plate off the table and said, 'Yes please!'

The kitchen was at the back of the house and one corner of it had been divided from the rest of the room by a wooden partition wall to form a tiny bathroom with just enough room for a bathtub and a small chair. I was having the only bath I remember having in there before I went into hospital to have the baby when a mouse ran across the floor and frightened me half to death. After that, I washed in the basin in the bedroom every morning, as the other girls did. I hated having to wash when there were other people in the room, but it was a choice between learning to overcome my shyness and come to terms with the erosion of what remained of my dignity or not washing at all. So I soon got used to it.

There was no sitting room in the house – at least, none that the girls were allowed to use – and there were no comfortable chairs to relax in. In the afternoons, we'd have a rest on our beds and then return to the dining room to wait for our tea, which consisted of bread and jam and, occasionally, a slice of cake. After tea, we usually stayed in the dining room, sitting around the table on hard wooden dining chairs, listening to the radio and waiting for the hours to pass. We didn't chat and 'bond', as young people would probably do today; when we did talk to each other, it was in a very desultory manner. In fact, none of us had any real enthusiasm for anything, and having listened to the radio and maybe flicked through a magazine in a half-hearted way, I'd be happy to go to bed.

We did the same thing every evening, and it's what we were doing on the evening of 15 August 1950, when the programme we were listening to was interrupted by the announcement that Princess Elizabeth, heir to the throne and oldest child of King George VI and Elizabeth Bowes-Lyon, the Duchess of York, had given birth at Clarence House in London earlier that day to a daughter weighing six pounds.

Breaking our customary silence, one of the girls sighed and said, 'Ah, she's had a little girl. That's nice.' She meant it in exactly the way she said it. I don't think any of us even thought to compare the very different circumstances surrounding the birth of Princess Elizabeth's child and our own; we certainly didn't feel bitter about it. For me, at least, that was probably partly because the baby I was carrying inside me wasn't real to me and I felt no more connected to it than I did to little Princess Anne Elizabeth Alice Louise. It wasn't going to be my child for more than a few weeks, so it was far better to remain detached and indifferent towards it.

9

I didn't know anything at all about what was involved in giving birth and I didn't really want to know. Like being at the home, it was something that had to be endured before I could move on with my life. Nothing could be done to change what was about to happen, so the only thing I could do was get through each day as best I could and remind myself at the end of it that I was one day closer to walking away from it all.

I didn't have any negative feelings towards the baby that was growing inside me. It was going to be born and there were things I was going to have to do that I didn't need to think about until I actually had to do them. Then I'd leave the home – alone, as I had been when I'd arrived – and go back to Rotherham, where I hoped I'd be able to carry on with the life I'd been leading nine months earlier.

With all of that in mind, I settled quite quickly into daily life at the home. Every day was pretty much the same as the previous one and as the one that came after it. The routine was only broken occasionally, for example when we had a visit after lunch one day from the local vicar.

We all sat round the table in the dining room while he talked. I can't remember what it was all about, except that at one point he mentioned the Father, the Son and the

Holy Spirit. When I raised my hand and asked him how the Holy Trinity was formed, he looked at me for a moment with his eyebrows slightly raised as if he thought I was being facetious. When he realized that the question was a serious one, he said, 'Ah, yes, well. It's a very good question. However, it's something I didn't really want to get into this week.' He raised his hand to cover his mouth and gave a little cough. 'We can talk about it another time.' But he didn't come again and my 'very good question' remained unanswered for many years.

The first time I went outside the home after I'd arrived was on the Sunday, when, led by the two women, we all walked, two abreast – a crocodile of pregnant girls – through the streets to a nearby church. It felt like taking part in some horrible walk of shame, and even though I kept my head down and my eyes focused on the ground in front of me, I knew people were watching us and I could hear the disapproving clicks of their tongues.

When we stepped out of the summer sunshine, through the arched doorway into the cool, dim light inside the church, one of the women led the way to a pew about halfway down the aisle. I sat there with my cheeks burning, my fists clenched tightly on my lap and my head lowered once again, this time so that I couldn't see the smirking faces of the choir boys. I could still hear them giggling and sniggering though, and I could hear snatches of what they were whispering to each other from behind raised hymn books.

Sitting in the church that day was a dreadful, appalling experience that made me feel more miserable than I'd done at any time since my brother Eric had shouted at me and disowned me. I understood that we were supposed to feel ashamed and realize we were wicked and full of sin, but all I really felt was degraded and resentful.

The same thing occurred the following Sunday, when I kept telling myself, 'I just have to get through this. It isn't long now and it'll all be over. I just have to grit my teeth and hold on.' And at least, after those visits to church, being restricted to the home didn't seem such a bad thing after all.

There was just one other occasion before my baby was born when I went outside the home; it was on the day my mother came to see me.

By the time I'd got pregnant, my mother and I really had no relationship at all. So I can't imagine why I felt homesick and asked her to visit me. Perhaps I needed to believe that I belonged *somewhere* and *someone* cared about me. Whatever the reason, I wrote to tell her that we were allowed to have visitors during a two-hour period on Saturday afternoons and I asked if she'd come one Saturday to see me. I clearly hadn't lost all sense of reality, however, and I enclosed some money for her bus fare from Rotherham to Huddersfield. Despite the added incentive, I hadn't really expected her to come, and I was surprised as well as delighted when I received a letter from her a few days later saying she would.

When the day arrived, I sat in the dining room after lunch with my eyes fixed on the window, watching the bit of road I could see beyond the front garden and waiting for two o'clock. When there was still no sign of her by two thirty, I went in search of the two women and told them, 'I think my mother must be having difficulty finding the house. Can I walk down the road as far as the bus stop and see if I can see her?' When they agreed, I almost flew out of the front door.

Unfortunately, the little I could remember about the day I'd arrived at the home almost three weeks earlier didn't include which way I'd walked when I'd got off the bus. I set off in what I hoped was the right direction and had only gone a short distance when I saw a bus stop I thought I recognized. There was no sign of my mother, however, so I continued to walk along the road, glancing down every side street as I went. And then I saw a pub.

Some instinct told me that my mother was in the pub, and although I wanted to see her, I stood on the street outside it for a moment, trying to decide what to do. Eventually, I pushed open the door just far enough to be able to see into the bar. And there she was, laughing as she lowered a glass of Guinness from her lips and then turning her head to smile at Ernie Burns.

I felt sick with disappointment. It was bad enough that she'd gone to a pub in the first place rather than walking up the road to see me when she must have known I'd be waiting for her. But I couldn't believe she'd brought *him* with her. Of course, when I thought about it afterwards, I realized I should have known that's exactly what she'd do: if she was going to travel twenty miles by bus from Rotherham to Huddersfield, she'd need to have some incentive other than simply visiting me – an incentive such as an afternoon out with Ernie Burns.

I was still standing in the doorway, trying not to cry, when she looked across and saw me. Fortunately, she was standing quite close to the door and although she didn't make any move towards me, I didn't have to go right into the pub for her to be able to hear me when I whispered, 'Aren't you going to come? It's just that . . . Well, visiting time's going on and . . .'

'Yeah, yeah.' She waved an irritably dismissive hand in my direction. 'I'll come when I've finished my drink.'

I took a step backwards so that I could close the door and then I stood outside the pub again, waiting and hoping I hadn't annoyed her so much she'd decide to catch the bus home without talking to me. She did come out after a while – thankfully without Ernie Burns, who remained in the pub drinking while she followed me, silently and resentfully, up the road.

When I rang the bell on the front door of the home, it was opened almost immediately by the more severe of the two women, who greeted my mother with cold politeness and spoke to her in a tone resonant with distaste. It was disapproval that was completely lost on my mother, who accepted the cup of tea that was offered to her and then sat with me in the dining room while I tried to think of something to say to her.

My mother had plenty to say, however, and as I sat looking out of the window on to the front garden, she complained about how long the bus journey had been; told me what she could have been doing on a Saturday afternoon that would have been infinitely preferable to having to traipse 'halfway across the country' for what she called 'no good reason'; and bemoaned the fact that she was now going to have to get another bus all the way back to Rotherham.

She didn't mention Ernie Burns and neither did I. Nor did I mention the fact that she seemed to have been having a nice enough time when I'd found her in the pub. And it wasn't long before I began to glance at the clock, as she'd been doing ever since she sat down in the dining room. It had been stupid of me to think her visit would be anything other than the horrible, embarrassing charade it turned out to be, and I was as relieved as she was when she eventually stood up and said that it was time for her to go.

She left without having spoken one single kind word to me, although as I watched her scuttle down the path and out of the gate without a backward glance, I knew I was the one who was responsible for the crushing disappointment I felt. Why had I thought things would be any different? For eighteen years, she'd had as little direct contact with me as she could get away with, and in all that time she'd never had a pleasant word to say to me. So why did I think she'd want to see me or have anything to say to me now? I should have known when I asked her to come and sent her money for the bus fare that she'd see it as an opportunity for a day out drinking with Ernie Burns. I wanted to believe that she'd intended to come straight to the home, but when she'd got off the bus and seen the pub it had proved too much of a temptation for her. However, that didn't explain the fact that she'd brought Ernie Burns with her, or her very obvious desire to get away from me and back to him as soon as she possibly could.

I felt stupid for allowing myself to believe she might want to visit me – although I suppose if I *had* truly believed that, I wouldn't have sent her money for the bus fare. The truth was that nothing had changed: she didn't have an ounce of maternal instinct in her whole body and she had no interest in me; all she was interested in was Ernie Burns, drinking and doing whatever else she wanted to do. After her brief and reluctant visit, I felt even more hurt and humiliated than I'd done before. I wouldn't make the same mistake again.

A couple of days later, I started having stomach pains. Although I knew almost nothing about childbirth, I was pretty sure that going into labour three weeks before my due date wasn't a good thing to be happening, and I was frightened. For the rest of the afternoon, I was checked regularly and watched over by the two women until eventually, in the evening, one of them phoned for an ambulance and I was taken to hospital.

What lay ahead for me was daunting and I was scared, but I was happy to be leaving the home and relieved to feel that I was one step closer to the end of the whole ordeal.

At the hospital, I was checked over by a nurse, then a midwife and finally a doctor. And then the pains stopped.

'The doctor wants to keep you in overnight,' the nurse told me. 'Although it seems to have been a false alarm, he wants to make sure everything's all right before he sends you home.'

I didn't know if she or the doctor knew that the 'home' they'd have been sending me back to was a Church of England home for unmarried mothers. I thought at the time that they didn't, although afterwards I realized that all the staff at the hospital must have known and it was their policy to treat everyone with kindness and respect, whatever their circumstances.

The next morning I was examined again by a nurse, then a midwife and then a different doctor, whose expression was serious but whose eyes seemed to be smiling as he told me, 'I think we'd better keep you here a bit longer – for a few more days – just to be on the safe side. Would that be all right with you?'

'Yes, that's fine,' I answered, trying not to sound as delighted as I felt. Spending a few nights almost anywhere would have been preferable to going back to the home; spending them somewhere where people were friendly and nice to me and where the air didn't smell of furniture polish and disapproval was more than I could have hoped for.

Despite the fact that the pains didn't return, I stayed in the hospital for the next three weeks, until my baby was born. I know without any shadow of doubt that the doctor allowed me to stay there because he'd taken pity on me, and to this day I'm grateful to him for his kindness. Instead of having to spend those last three weeks feeling lonely and being reminded constantly of my sinful ways, I was treated like all the other expectant mums, I had people to talk to and, for the first time in weeks, I was able to relax and feel at ease.

The labour ward I'd been admitted to when I'd arrived at the hospital had six beds, three along each of its two longer walls, and a delivery room at one end of it. Every day for the next three weeks, women arrived on the ward in labour, had their babies and then moved on – except for one woman who gave birth on the bed right next to mine before they could get her into the delivery room.

I spent my days reading, talking and laughing with the other women, and feeling 'normal'. Occasionally, someone would ask me about my husband and why he hadn't been in to visit me. The first time it happened, I hesitated and could feel my cheeks burning with embarrassment as I said, 'I haven't got a husband. I . . . I'm not married.' I didn't know which would be worse: if the woman simply refused to speak to me again, or if she said something coldly censorious. I was taken aback by her reaction, which was to nod, as if what I'd said had been ordinary and unremarkable, and then ask me, 'So when's your baby due?'

Every single person who asked me about my husband while I was in hospital reacted in a similar way when I gave them the truthful answer; not one of them showed any sign of disapproval or gave any indication that they were judging me. It was a revelation and a source of great comfort to me. To those women, the fact that we were all in the same boat – waiting to give birth or already having done so – was the only thing that really mattered.

The hospital staff didn't seem to make judgements either – at least, none they allowed to affect the way they treated me. It was the second time in my life when being in hospital proved to be better than being at home – and it was considerably better than being in the home for unmarried mothers. When I did eventually go into labour, very close to my due date, there were unbridled cheers all round.

I'd seen so many newborn babies by that time that I was more or less prepared for what was going to happen. Some of the babies who'd been born to women who'd passed through the ward during the weeks I was there were very sweet; some of them probably just needed a few days to 'grow into themselves'! Oddly, perhaps, I didn't connect any of them with the baby I was carrying. I didn't really think of it as a real person at all.

The pains started in the early hours of a Friday morning – 17 September 1950. I'd been moved several days earlier into a small side ward, and when it was confirmed that I really was in labour this time, they moved me back into the labour ward. Then, during the afternoon, I was finally taken to the delivery room.

It's amazing how soon after giving birth the memory of the pain and of your complete and utter conviction that you will never, ever, do it again, fades. I seemed to be in labour for hours, and one thing I do remember with clarity is being told to 'push' for what seemed like the hundredth time. I remember too, just as another massive wave of agony threatened to carry me away with it, thinking, 'I wish my mother was here.' That shows how bad it was: clearly, I was delirious!

I was certainly frightened, and almost totally unprepared for the pain. Sweat was dripping from every inch of my body and I was just about to shout at anyone who might be able to hear me that I didn't think I *could* push again, when I heard a cry. It was very weak at first, and then it gradually increased in strength and volume until it sounded like the call of a small, furious seagull.

'It's a girl!' The nurse whose fingers I'd earlier been crushing in a vice-like grip took hold of my hand again and gave it a squeeze. Then someone put the baby in my arms and as I looked down into the large blue eyes that seemed to be looking directly into mine, I knew, with more certainty than I'd ever known anything in my life, that I couldn't give her away.

I didn't say anything to anyone about what I'd decided. I had no idea how I was going to manage to keep her; I just knew that, however impossible it seemed, that was what I was going to do. The only other thing I was certain of at that time was that I'd have a tremendous battle on my hands trying to persuade my mother to see my point of view. But this was *my* child, and I knew that whatever problems and difficulties I was going to have to face, nothing on earth could make me give her away and go home without her.

I don't know whether the nurses at the hospital were aware that my baby was going to be adopted. If they were, they certainly didn't give any indication of it.

'She weighs seven pounds four ounces,' one of the nurses told me.

'Is that normal?' I asked anxiously. 'Is that what a baby *should* weigh?'

The nurse laughed and patted my shoulder as she answered, 'I'd say that it was just about perfect.'

'Have you got a name for her?' another nurse asked.

I hadn't thought about names at all: since discovering I was pregnant, I hadn't wanted to do anything that would make the baby real. Suddenly, giving her a name seemed very important.

'No! I haven't got a name for her,' I said. 'I need to think of one.'

'Well –' the nurse looked down at the tiny head resting in the crook of my arm '– what about Linda?'

'I don't think she's a Linda,' I said.

'Barbara's nice.' The other nurse smiled at me from where she was standing at the foot of the bed.

'No, not Barbara either.'

Valerie, Sharon, Sandra – the nurses were doing their best, and although all the names they thought of were nice, none of them seemed to suit the baby I was holding in my arms. Then the name Patricia popped into my head and I knew instantly that it was right. I almost decided on Patricia Anne, but she was going to have my surname, Manns – the name of the man who wasn't really my father – and Anne Manns is a bit of a tongue-twister. So she ended up as just Patricia, a name that still suits her perfectly.

Now all I had to do was find a way to clothe, feed and take care of her for the next eighteen years.

I remained in hospital for about a week after Pat was born and although my mother came to see me, she didn't stay very long and she didn't seem to be able to think of anything very much to say to me.

'Pat's beautiful, Mam,' I told her. 'She's upstairs in the nursery. When you've seen her, will you come back here?'

'I don't want to see her,' my mother answered brusquely. 'Anyway, I can't stop long. I've got to . . .' She paused and it was clear that she was trying to think of an excuse not to stay. In the end she said, lamely, 'I've got to get the bus back home.'

'I want to keep the baby.' I blurted the words out before I lost my nerve completely and she left without my having said them. 'Can I bring her home, Mam? I can't let her be adopted. I've got to keep her. Please, Mam.'

'No!' My mother looked at me at last, but with an expression of shocked distaste. 'Of course you can't bring her home; definitely not. Don't be stupid.' A few minutes later she left, without having seen her granddaughter.

My mother still seemed to believe that none of our neighbours or anyone else in Rotherham knew I'd been pregnant. She was ashamed of me and, in addition to her strong aversion to anything that might cause her any inconvenience, I think it was the thought of people finding out that made the idea of my going home with a baby so horrifying to her – as if she hadn't brought enough shame on the family herself by carrying on with Ernie Burns for all those years! If that *is* the explanation, it rather falls apart in light of what she told my boss.

Before I left Rotherham, I'd given my manager at the National Assistance Board the letter my doctor had written stating that I couldn't work because I had a growth in my stomach, and one day, when I was in the home in Huddersfield, he paid a visit to the house in Eastwood Lane to see how I was getting on. That was when my mother explained to him what was really 'wrong' with me and where I was. She told some very big lies in her life – to herself as well as to other people – so why she didn't lie to him then I don't know. Despite telling him the truth, however, she seemed happy to go on believing that no one else knew.

Even today, I don't understand how she was able to separate so completely what I'd done just once from what she was doing several times a week every week for years with a married man. The affair that had begun before I was born was still going on when my older brothers were courting and after they were married. It must have been humiliating for them to know that the girls they were bringing home would eventually discover what was happening. The truth was that although quick to condemn other people for their wrongdoings, my mother considered herself to be beyond criticism. In her eyes, she was entitled to do what she wanted simply because *she* wanted to do it. If any of her children ever gave any indication that they were uncomfortable about her relationship with Ernie Burns, her attitude was always 'Put up [with it] or shut up'.

I hadn't seen a great deal of my sister Mabel while I was pregnant. She was working and so was I, and although she was the only person I might have been able to talk to, I'd felt ashamed of my predicament and perhaps, too, that I'd let her down. I wrote to her when I was in the hospital after Pat was born and told her that my baby was beautiful and I was going to keep her, although I didn't know how I was going to manage it because our mother had said I couldn't take her home.

When I left hospital with Pat and went back to the home for unmarried mothers, the other girls didn't ask any questions about why I'd been away for so long, but they did want to see my baby and they said nice things about her. Pat slept in a cot that had been placed beside my bed in the room I shared with Annie and Mavis and, relieved from most house-cleaning duties, my days now revolved around feeding and caring for her.

At the back of the house there was a cobbled stone courtyard lined by what had once been stables and by some other outbuildings, one of which had been converted into a laundry room. Few people had washing machines in 1950 and everything – including soiled nappies – had to be washed by hand in cold water in the stone sink.

The worst thing about using the laundry room – even worse than the red soreness of your swollen hands after

This is a rare photograph: my mother almost has a smile on her face! I'm wearing a new dress, a very pretty pale green one, which was rather special to me and which I loved so much. Eddie's wearing what at that time was his usual sulky pout; he was eighteen months old.

My handsome brother Eric (before he
disowned me), me at about sixteen years old,
and my mother – who never smiled much!

Me at the age of sixteen.

A photograph taken on my
twenty-first birthday.

This photograph, which was taken by a friend, was the first one of Pat and me together and the first one ever taken of Pat, who's about six months old.

Pat is one year old and able to sit unsupported.

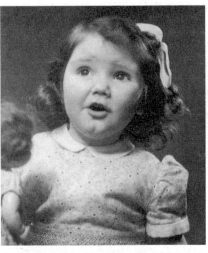

Pat was entertained by the photographer, who was throwing a ball up into the air; this photograph was taken as it was coming down.

Pat and I were on holiday in Torquay with my brother Eddie and his fiancée Iris. I was their chaperone! It was all so exciting for Pat and we were both having a really great time.

This is so typical of Pat when she is near sand; to this day she heartily dislikes it and much prefers a pebble beach.

Another photograph taken on our holiday in Torquay.
With the constant excitement and so many new things to do,
it was no wonder Pat fell asleep.

Droopy Drawers. This photograph
of Pat was taken at the bungalow
in Billericay.

This was taken when I was twenty-
four years old, just before my marriage
to Roy. The dress was meant to be
worn on my wedding day but wasn't,
because of Roy's plan on the day.

Peter starting school at the age of five. The photographer provided the panda!

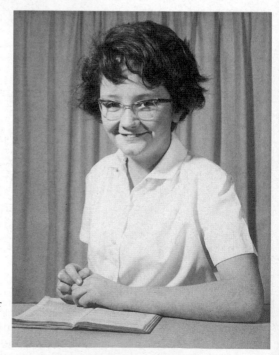

A school photo of Pat aged twelve.

Pat and Chris's wedding day. It was August 1970 and the fashions were fantastic, especially if you had a great pair of legs!

Eddie and me on a trip to North Yorkshire.

Pat and Peter spending a convivial evening together.

Peter and me introducing Harriet to her new sister
Clarissa, in May 1995.

This photo shows all the caring, loving ways my husband
Austin had. The love shines through.

you'd plunged them repeatedly into icy-cold water – was being the first person in the morning to use the scrubbing brush. Picking it up very carefully between two fingers, you'd hold it out at arm's length, take a deep breath, shake it and then watch with disgust as dozens of little black insects came swarming out of its bristles, scurried across the wooden draining board and disappeared into cracks in the wall. In retrospect, having to do all those household chores before the birth didn't seem so bad now: little had I thought I'd ever miss polishing the hall floor and doing battle with the 'bumper'.

I didn't tell anyone at the home that I was going to keep Pat. Just thinking about all the obstacles I was going to have to face and overcome made me feel sick with anxiety, so I didn't want to hear all the arguments against it. And then I received a letter from my sister.

Mabel had always been good to me, and over the last few years her role as surrogate mother had changed and she'd become my friend. In reality, she was my half-sister, although to me she was always simply 'my sister'. Even when I became pregnant and my brother Eric turned his back on me and refused to speak to me, Mabel's attitude towards me didn't change in any way. She was the one person who'd always loved and supported me. I'd always known she was a decent, kind person; it wasn't until I received her letter that I understood just how good she really was – and her husband, Bill, too.

'Bill and I have talked it over,' she wrote, 'and we could look after Pat from Monday to Friday every week. Then you could pick her up after work on Friday and have her with you for the weekend. Of course, Mam would have to agree to it.'

Mabel and Bill had three teenagers and a four-year-old at that time, so they already had their hands full without having to look after a baby as well. I couldn't believe what they were offering to do for me and for Pat. When I'd written to Mabel from the hospital, it hadn't even crossed my mind that she'd be able or willing to help me. I kept reading her letter over and over again, trying to absorb the fact that she was prepared to take care of Pat during the week, thereby solving what had appeared to be an insoluble problem.

I was over the moon – until I remembered that the plan was still only a plan. Everything now rested on getting my mother's agreement to allow me to have Pat at home at the weekends – and that was likely to prove to be the biggest, most insurmountable problem of them all.

On the Saturday after I came out of hospital, my mother visited me at the home in Huddersfield, this time without being begged to do so, and on that occasion she did look at her granddaughter. She didn't say anything: she just looked briefly into the cot and then turned away.

With shaking hands and a thudding heart, I showed her Mabel's letter. She read it without comment and then dropped it on to the table beside her.

'Please, Mam,' I begged her. 'Please can I come home with Pat?' And this time she said, 'I'll think about it,' which was so far removed from the flat 'no' I'd been expecting that I almost dared to hope it might actually happen.

I didn't know until later, but my mother had already

been given reason to reconsider her previously adamant refusal to acknowledge publicly the fact that I'd been pregnant. One of the two people who spoke openly to her was our neighbour in Eastwood Lane, who we called Auntie Alice, who asked her one day, 'Has your Sheila had her baby yet?' My mother must have been very surprised to discover that the carefully kept secret wasn't a secret at all. I can't imagine what she said in response to Auntie Alice's next question though, which was, 'Whatever made you send the poor girl away?'

It was to my mother's sister, my Auntie Gerty, that I owed a debt of gratitude for finally closing any debate when she told my mother, 'If you don't have that girl home with her baby, I will never speak to you again.' (Her other sister, my Auntie Marion, had died just after the war from a tumour on the brain.)

The next week, my mother visited me again and when I summoned the courage to ask her if she'd thought any more about letting me go home with Pat, she said, 'Yes, OK.'

I was terrified of doing or saying anything that might make her change her mind, and it was with a sense of rising panic that I asked her, 'Can I go home with you now? I mean, there's no need for me to stay here, is there, if I'm not going to have Pat adopted? Will you go and ask if I can go home with you today?'

My mother's voice was irritable again as she said, 'If you want to leave, you go and ask them yourself.'

I didn't *ask* them: I didn't dare risk the possibility that they might say 'no'. I took a deep breath, knocked on the door of the office and said, more loudly than I'd intended, in a voice that I hoped conveyed a confidence I didn't feel, 'I'm going to take Pat and go home with my mother today.'

To my surprise, the woman just nodded and said, 'OK.' I suppose there wasn't much else she *could* say; it wasn't a prison after all, and now that Pat wasn't going to be adopted, I was free to leave whenever I wanted to. 'When you've packed up your things, come back here and I'll give you your allowance book,' the woman told me, and then she smiled at me for first time since the day I'd arrived at the home.

Half an hour later, I was sitting on the bus beside my mother, holding my baby in my arms, on my way back to Rotherham to start a new life I couldn't even begin to imagine.

I was so anxious to get out of there I don't think I showed any sign of gratitude for what had been done for me. But I *was* grateful, to the two women and to the Church of England, for having taken me in after I'd transgressed against society, and for putting a roof over my head when my own mother didn't want me.

My brother Eric was at home when we arrived. I asked him if he wanted to look at his niece and he turned away from me and said coldly, 'No, I don't. I expect I'll see plenty of her in the future.' Although I hadn't expected the house to be decorated with bunting and banners welcoming me home, I felt very sad when I realized that Eric still couldn't forgive me. And neither, it seemed, could God.

When I came home I wanted Pat to be christened, so I

made an appointment to meet the vicar of St Stephen's Church, which was at the bottom of the road where we lived. I'd expected him to talk about what christening meant in religious terms and about the practical arrangements that needed to be made. Instead, his first words to me were, 'You do understand that you're a sinner and that you've committed a terrible sin against God?' Then he gave me a lecture, which reduced me to floods of tears.

He did agree in the end to christen Pat, although not until he felt assured that I appreciated the fact that what I'd done had blackened my soul and reduced my value as a human being in his eyes, in the eyes of society as a whole and, it seemed, in the eyes of God. I believed he was right; I just hadn't expected him to be quite so harsh in his criticism.

The welfare state (and the NHS) had only been in existence for two years, since 1948, and it had been set up to provide for men, not women – it wasn't until 1970 that women were paid the same as men doing the same job, and it was five years after that when it became illegal to sack a woman for being pregnant.

State benefits were available – on the basis of a concept of social rights which meant that only men doing or prepared to do paid work were eligible for social welfare. In 1950, the state didn't provide financial or any other kind of assistance to single mothers. Mothers were expected to be married and to be supported by their husbands; when they became mothers, they were expected to stay at home and look after their children, at least until they started school at the age of five. There wasn't the range of pre-school care in the form of childminders, nurseries and crèches that there is today. If I was going to keep Pat, I had to work to support us both, and I couldn't have done that without Mabel's help.

There was certainly no chance of someone like me being given council accommodation. It was only five years since the war had ended and there were men who'd served their country who needed housing; even many of *them* had to wait on the council housing list for years while houses were being built. Nissen huts and Bellman hangars had been used during the war as accommodation for military personnel and similar types of buildings, known as 'prefabs', were built after the war to house some of the vast number of people who'd been made homeless by the bombing and others who were being rehoused as part of a post-war programme of slum clearance.

Assembled on site from factory-made components, prefabs were quickly constructed and relatively cheap. By 1950, almost 160,000 had been built in the UK. They were very popular amongst the people who lived in them, which included my eldest brother, John, and his wife Win, who moved into one when John left the steelworks at the end of the war and joined the police force.

When people got married, they put their names on the council housing list and lived with their parents or in-laws until something became available for them. It wasn't the norm at that time for young couples to *buy* houses – my brother Harry and his wife Olive were considered to be very bold and modern when they took out a mortgage and bought a little terraced house.

By the time I came home with Pat, all my brothers except Eric and Eddie had married and moved out. Eric and Eddie shared the back bedroom and I slept in the bedroom at the front of the house with my mother, and with Pat at the weekends. In our neighbourhood, someone always knew someone who was selling whatever you needed, and I'd been able to buy a cot and a second-hand pram for Pat.

I hadn't been home for very long when my sister-in-law Olive told me conversationally one day, 'I asked Harry if we could adopt Pat, seeing as we haven't been able to have any children of our own. But he said it wouldn't work out. He said that with us living so close to you, it wouldn't be nice for any of us.'

'I don't want anyone to adopt Pat,' I told her, aghast. 'I want to keep her.' I was bemused, although I don't think Olive even noticed. Olive is a lovely woman and I've always got on very well with her. I suppose she just assumed that having Pat was a 'problem' for me and that it would have been a help to me if she'd been able to solve the 'problem' while at the same time keeping Pat in the family. What she hadn't understood was that although there was a whole host of problems surrounding the practicalities of taking care of Pat, Pat herself wasn't a problem of any kind. To me, she was a blessing.

Fortunately, although Olive and Harry had almost given up hope of being able to have children of their own, they did eventually have a son and a daughter. I'm sure they realized then why I'd been so nonplussed by what Olive said to me that day.

*

Pat was three months old when I arranged to meet her father in Sheffield. I hadn't told him why I wanted to see him; I suspected later that he thought I'd been going to ask him if there was any possibility of starting up our relationship again. Nothing could have been further from the truth. The real reason for asking him to meet me was because I wanted him to see Pat. He'd told me he didn't want to see her, but it didn't seem right simply to ignore the child he'd been fifty per cent responsible for bringing into the world. I wasn't going to ask him to *do* anything for her, or for me; I just wanted him to look at her and to acknowledge her existence.

He was waiting for me at the bus stop when I got off the bus and at first he refused to look at Pat. Watching him standing there, angry and defensive, I couldn't remember what I'd ever seen in him or why I'd been flattered and beguiled into having sex with him, even once. I suppose it was the effect of chronic low self-esteem and having been jilted by someone who *was* decent and worth loving.

He did eventually look at the baby I was holding in my arms and, having done what I came to do, I turned away from him and got on a bus that would take me home to Rotherham. I didn't even see him walk away, and that was the first and last time he ever saw Pat.

Pat settled immediately into the weekly routine that quickly became established. Mabel and Bill lived with their children – and now, most of the time, with my child too – about three miles and a fourpence ha'penny bus ride out of town. I'd take Pat there every Sunday and then I'd make the journey again after work on Fridays to pick her up and take her home with me. It wasn't easy leaving her every week, although it would have been much harder if it had been with anyone other than my sister. There was no alternative: I had to work, to pay for everything Pat needed and to pay my mother for my room and board at home.

Unless they had independent financial means and the support of their family – which would have been relatively rare at that time – girls in my situation usually had no alternative other than to hand their babies over for adoption or to be cared for by the state. I was very aware of how fortunate I was to have Mabel and Bill, who were prepared to help me so that I *could* work and provide for myself and for Pat. I have to give my mother some credit too, because she could have refused to let me have Pat at home at weekends, and then I don't know what I'd have done. By some huge stroke of good fortune, after having been more or less indifferent to all her children, and particularly to her daughters, she really did love Pat and she quickly developed a bond with her that she'd certainly never had with any of us.

Going back to work was the first big step I had to take in what was going to be a very different sort of world for me from now on. As well as being apprehensive about how people would treat me, I was anxious to strike the right balance in terms of my own demeanour now that I was an unmarried mother. I didn't want to appear brazen, as if I didn't care what anyone thought about my situation;

at the same time, I didn't want to give people a stick to beat me with by giving the impression that I was demoralized and oppressed by my changed circumstances. I knew I'd be treading a fine line and I was dreading being ridiculed and ostracized.

I was very lucky that my old job at the National Assistance Board had been kept open for me. Perhaps they'd known all along what the 'growth in my stomach' really was, or at least had guessed the truth when I put on a lot of weight and then departed so abruptly. Believing that they didn't know had certainly been easier for me at the time. However, I was very nervous about going back to work there, and particularly about how people would react to my reappearance.

I worked in an office with one other woman and several men; it was my job to type up the notes they made when they went out on visits to people's homes. They were all substantially older than I was and I was very afraid that they'd openly despise and disapprove of me. So it was a huge relief when they were nice to me and told me they were glad to see me back at work again.

Despite their kindness, having to face people was even more difficult than I'd thought it was going to be and I felt ill at ease all the time. I wanted people to accept me and treat me as if nothing had changed; but although I was proud of Pat, I wasn't proud of what I'd done. Perhaps the real problem was that I was finding it difficult to forgive myself. I just hoped things would get better in time, as I learned to deal with my new situation, and that I'd eventually stop dreading the moment I was always anticipating when someone would ask me an awkward, embarrassing question.

One day, when the woman I worked with was out of the office, one of the men told a dirty joke. It was something that had *never* happened before: older men didn't do that sort of thing in front of young women at that time. I could feel the colour rising into my cheeks as I sat at my desk, attempting to focus on the words that seemed to be moving across the piece of paper in the typewriter in front of me and trying not to show how upset I was.

Although I suppose I was overreacting because of the way I felt, it was almost as if someone had whispered in my ear, 'How could you have been stupid enough to think that things are still the way they used to be?' I already felt vulnerable because of my situation, and it seemed to me that when one of the men told a dirty joke and all the others laughed, it highlighted the fact that I'd lost any right to the respect I might previously have had. It was certainly true that they wouldn't have dreamed of telling a joke like that if the other woman had been in the office. The unspoken message seemed to be that as I'd had sex when I wasn't married, it didn't matter if they offended me.

It made me realize that everything had changed and nothing would ever be the same again. I knew immediately that I couldn't stay there any longer.

During my lunch hour a couple of days later, I went out to the shops to buy some knitting wool. I was still very keen on knitting, although since Pat's birth the Fair Isle jumpers and cardigans had largely given way to baby clothes, and on that day I wanted to buy some wool to make a matinee jacket. There was quite a large wool shop on the corner just down the road from the office. The young woman who worked in there was friendly and when she saw the knitting pattern and the wool I'd selected, she asked if I had a baby and I told her about Pat.

'My little boy's a bit younger,' she said. 'My mother looks after him so I can work. This is my husband's shop. I used to enjoy working here, but I want to stay at home now and look after my baby myself. I can't though, not until I can find someone to work here in my place.'

A few days later, after I'd been interviewed by the woman's husband and had left my job at the National Assistance Board, I started work at the wool shop.

Although I now had to work on Saturdays and therefore couldn't have Pat at home for the whole weekend, I only worked a half-day on Wednesdays, and as soon as I'd locked up the shop, I'd run to catch the bus to my sister's house in Hellaby to spend the afternoon with her.

The wool shop was in Attercliffe, which at that time

was a rundown part of Sheffield where people had very little money. There'd been a recent shortage of wool, followed by a sharp increase in its price, when the Americans had begun to stockpile it at the start of the Korean War in 1950. So the shop was never very busy.

When there weren't any customers, I was able to make myself a cup of tea using the kettle and gas ring in the shop's tiny, cramped basement. The problem was that the basement could only be accessed via a trapdoor in the middle of the shop floor and by climbing down the rungs of a narrow, steep ladder – which was fine if you weren't afraid of falling from the ladder or of an unwary customer crashing through the open trapdoor while you were down there. As both possibilities seemed very real to me, I only ventured down there a few times before deciding it was safer for all concerned if I bought my tea at the café next door.

It was while I was working at the wool shop that I went to see Pat one Wednesday afternoon and Mabel told me excitedly, 'Guess what? She said "Mamma" to me today!'

'Oh, that's . . . Did she? That's great.' I tried to sound pleased and to ignore the voice inside my head that was saying, 'No! That's not right. I don't want that. You're not her mother. I am.'

I wasn't seeing as much of Pat as I wanted to and although I wouldn't have hurt Mabel's feelings for all the world, in that moment I felt jealous of her and I knew I had to find a way of bringing Pat home to live with me.

It was wintertime when I started working at the wool shop and the small, single-barred gas fire had no impact at all on the icy air. I'd been told to keep the door of the shop open, but when swirling snowflakes began to blow in from outside, I closed it. The owner of the wool shop – who was a young man just a few years older than me – also owned a furniture store in Rotherham, which was where he spent most of his time. He often called in to see me on his way to and from there and later that morning the bell above the door jangled furiously and he came storming into the shop.

'You *do not* shut this door!' he shouted at me. 'I thought I told you that it must be left open at all times.'

'Oh, I'm sorry,' I told him. 'It started to snow and I was really cold.'

'Well, that's too bad,' he countered. 'The door stays open.'

The following Saturday, I woke up early with a very nasty cold and a high temperature. Dragging myself out of bed, I went to the doctor who gave me a certificate that would enable me to stay off work and wrote a prescription for me to take to the chemist. By the time I was standing in line at the pharmacy waiting to be served, I felt so ill I nearly passed out. I had to go to a phone box to call my boss and let him know I wouldn't be able to go in to work that day, but when I stopped in first at the house, he'd already arrived to pick up the keys to the shop from me.

He could see how ill I was. I explained to him what had happened and that I was about to go out to phone him, and he just held out his hand, saying, 'Keys.' Then he turned on his heels and left. Monday morning's post brought a letter from him telling me that as I hadn't been there on time to open the shop on the Saturday, I was sacked, with immediate effect and without any pay in lieu of notice.

I was extremely upset. I *needed* that job: how was I going to support myself and Pat without it? It seemed so mean and unjust of him to have sacked me like that, when he'd seen for himself that I was genuinely ill and when he knew I'd been doing a good, conscientious job at the shop. In fact, I was so incensed that I decided to go and see a solicitor and tell him what had happened. Making bold decisions was starting to become a habit. Perhaps making one really major one – as I'd done when I decided to keep Pat – acts like breath being blown on the smouldering ashes of your self-esteem.

'He didn't even mention the wages that are owed to me,' I told the solicitor indignantly. 'And he didn't give me a chance to work out my notice. I think he should have paid me, shouldn't he?'

'Yes,' the solicitor answered. 'He certainly should have done. I'm sure he knows that. I'll write him a letter.'

A few days later, a letter arrived in the post for me from the solicitor asking me to make an appointment to go and see him to collect my money. The owner of the wool shop had paid up – five pounds, which was a whole week's wages. Although it doesn't sound very much now, it was a lot in 1950, when a loaf of bread cost about four (old) pence. In fact, it was enough to pay my mother for my keep *and* my sister for looking after Pat for an entire week.

When I asked the solicitor what I owed him for writing the letter and getting the money for me, he smiled and said, 'You don't owe me anything. It was a pleasure to do it for you. I wouldn't have felt that justice had been served if I'd allowed that man to get away with treating you the way he did, particularly considering your circumstances.'

I thought that was very nice of him. Society might have condemned single mothers, but some people went out of their way to help me – not only the solicitor, but the bosses at George Cohen's, who'd kept me on when they knew I was pregnant, and my employers at the National Assistance Board, where my job had been kept open for me while I was away in Huddersfield having Pat.

Now all I had to do was find another job. Fortunately, the early 1950s were a period of high productivity in Britain and the Sheffield/Rotherham area was awash with small – as well as some very large – manufacturing companies. There were steelworks and rolling mills producing steel for the motor and aircraft industries, for mining and shipbuilding, and a whole plethora of other industries that have since declined and, in many cases, disappeared completely.

When I went to the local Labour Exchange, I found a job immediately as a typist at a steelworks called W. T. Flather, which was in Tinsley, on the road between Rotherham and Sheffield. I was happy to be back to working five days a week and being able to have Pat at home with me for the whole weekend.

Pat was really coming on well. My mother and Eddie were very fond of her. My other brothers and their wives were too, and they always took an interest in her when they came to visit my mother from time to time. It was just Eric who still ignored her, and me. Although he had a lady in his life by that time, love didn't seem to have mellowed him at all as far as we were concerned. When he got married and left to set up home with his new wife, the atmosphere in our house changed completely.

I often took Pat to see Auntie Gerty – the one who'd told my mother she'd never speak to her again if she didn't allow me to bring my baby home. I loved going to Auntie Gerty's house. She never asked questions or made me feel guilty or ashamed; she simply accepted me and Pat the way we were and she was kind to us. Both my mother's sisters were like that; I don't know what had happened, if anything, to make my mother so different from them.

When I was working for W. T. Flather, my mother had a job as a cleaner in the offices at the Magistrates' Court, which must have been what prompted her to say to me one day, 'Pat's father should be contributing towards her upkeep. I think you should take him to court.' Her advice wasn't always sound, to put it mildly, but what she said on that occasion did seem to make sense.

I didn't want to be involved with Pat's father for any reason. On the other hand, I *was* struggling to manage on what I was earning and I knew my mother was right about one thing she'd said to me: I owed it to Pat to do my best for her – although it seemed ironic to have to be reminded of that by my mother, of all people!

Eventually, after thinking about it for some time, I decided to go ahead and apply through the court for maintenance for Pat. Her father wasn't very happy when he found out what I'd done. He wrote me a letter pleading with me, 'Don't go through the courts, please. I'll pay the money directly to you.' Some instinct told me that he wouldn't and, in any case, it was already too late. Once I'd taken that first step, the judicial process had begun and after forms had been filled in, applications had been made, more forms had been filled in, and then the court ordered him to pay one pound a week towards the cost of bringing up his child.

It wasn't a lot of money, even then, but it was a great help – or, at least, it would have been if he'd paid it regularly. In fact, he rarely paid it at all, and after a while he applied to the court to have the weekly amount reduced to fifteen shillings, which he often still failed to pay.

I'd been trying to think of some way of having Pat living at home with me all week when I heard about a nursery where children could be looked after while their mothers were at work. It was a fairly 'modern' concept at the time; I certainly didn't know of anything similar. Mothers didn't work outside the home in the 1950s – or even very much in the 1960s – and there were no state pre-schools or nurseries as there are now. I didn't even know how much it would cost or whether it was a practical idea at all when I plucked up the courage one day to ask my mother, 'If I can get Pat into this nursery I've heard about, can she come to live here?' I asked. And, to my amazement, she said 'Yes'.

When I made an appointment to go to the nursery to talk to the woman who ran it, I didn't know if there was a place available. I was elated when it turned out that there was and that Pat could have it. The cost of one shilling a day would include all Pat's food while she was there, which at that time was primarily Ostermilk. It was a price I could pay out of what I was earning. I could hardly believe it.

Now all I had to do was tell Mabel. It was a task I was dreading because I knew Mabel had grown to love Pat. So I was hugely relieved and grateful when she said she completely understood and that she was happy for me. My little girl really was going to be able to come home and live with me.

Pat was just under a year old when she started at the nursery. She settled in very quickly and was happy there. Every morning I walked into town, pushing her in the pram, caught a bus to the nursery, left her there, got the bus back to the town centre and then caught another to Tinsley, where I worked. In the evening, I repeated the same journey in reverse. It quickly became my routine and it didn't seem like a chore at all, because I had Pat.

She stayed at that nursery until she was four, and for those three years I was able to go to work every day knowing she was safe and being well cared for. As well as the woman who ran the nursery, there were three or four very nice girls who looked after the children, who were all ages. Pat learned a lot while she was there: listening to her recite the nursery rhymes they taught her, complete with all the actions, would have melted all but the hardest heart. Sadly, Eric remained unmoved.

The problem was that because Pat was so sweet and lovable, it was difficult for me to discipline her or give her even a mild telling-off. It wasn't because of Pat herself; it was due to the fact that whenever I so much as grumbled at her, my mother and my brother Eddie would get angry with *me*. They both adored her, and my mother – who'd always complained so bitterly and vociferously about her own children and had thought up all sorts of ways to get them out from under her feet – was often heard to say how nice it was to have a little one in the house again!

On Mondays to Fridays, my daily routine involved taking Pat to the nursery, going to work, picking her up again, going home, feeding her, bathing her and putting her to bed. On Saturdays, Pat and I would go to visit my aunt, my sister or one of my brothers, and then sometimes in the evening I'd go to the cinema with Jean, the girl who'd told everyone at George Cohen Sons & Co. the secret I'd confided in her when I became pregnant. Surprisingly, perhaps, we'd remained friends, primarily because her parents were very kind to Pat. On Sundays, while my mother went to the pub with Ernie Burns, I stayed at home and cooked the lunch, as I'd been doing since I was eleven years old.

One day after Pat had been at the nursery for a few months, I arrived to pick her up after work and the woman in charge told me, 'I'm rather concerned that Pat doesn't have any warm clothes. Winter's coming – the days are already getting quite chilly – and what she's wearing isn't warm enough.'

I was very embarrassed and ashamed. How had I not realized that Pat's clothes weren't at all suitable for the changed weather? I suppose the answer was that I hadn't ever had different clothes for winter and summer. When I was a child, there was never any money to spare and I wore whatever my mother gave me to wear; if it didn't fit or it wasn't appropriate for cold weather, it was just too bad. I had a new pair of shoes once a year, at Whitsuntide, and when their soles became worn and full of holes, my mother gave me a piece of cardboard to stuff inside them. It didn't stop my socks and feet getting wet when it rained; it just slowed the process slightly, made the shoes even tighter and more uncomfortable, and produced a squelching sound whenever I took a step. However, what I hadn't had as a child wasn't an excuse for not making sure Pat had the clothes she needed, and I was mortified at the thought that someone else had had to point that out to me.

Once I'd been made aware of Pat's need for warmer clothing, the problem became finding the money to buy it. After I'd paid for everything that had to be paid for every week, there was almost no money left over. So although I told the woman who ran the nursery that of course I'd get Pat everything she needed, the truth was that I didn't know how I was going to do it.

It was our neighbour Nellie who came to the rescue. Nellie did a lot of sewing and when I confided in her one day that Pat needed warm clothes and I didn't know how I was going to afford to buy them, she dismissed my anxiety with a shrug of her shoulders and said, 'Well, why don't you make them?'

'I like sewing,' I told her. 'But I've never made a garment.'

'It's simple,' she laughed. 'Just buy a pattern, follow the instructions and you can't go wrong.'

My mother helped me pick out some Viyella material and the first thing I made was a dress for Pat. It was to be the first of many. Then, one day, I was visiting my mother's sister, Auntie Gerty, when she told me, 'Someone I know is selling her old sewing machine for thirty shillings. If I lend you the money to buy it, you can pay me back half a crown a week.' It was typical of my aunt to offer to do something like that; she was always very kind to me. It would take me twelve weeks to repay the debt, but Pat *had* to have clothes to wear and it *was* a good deal. So I agreed.

It was an ancient, German-made hand sewing machine with a torpedo shuttle and no instruction notes. I soon worked it out though, and before long Pat was the warmest, best-dressed child at the nursery! That old sewing machine continued to give sterling service for many years, and I used it to make almost all Pat's clothes and my own.

I did occasionally buy clothes for Pat though. There was a very nice shop in town that sold lovely things for babies and young children and I was walking past it one day when I noticed in the window a beautiful outfit of beige trousers and a little zip-up jacket made of (faux) fur. It was quite pricey – certainly more than I could afford – but I *had* to have it for Pat. Fortunately, the woman who ran the shop agreed to lay the outfit aside for me and let me pay for it weekly. When I made the last payment and took the jacket and trousers home with me, Pat looked lovely in them.

My brother Eric was married by that time and had a

child of his own. He still wouldn't talk to me or to Pat; if he was visiting our mother and I came into the room, he'd ignore me completely and continue to talk to her as if I wasn't there. Seeing Pat in that outfit did make him speak to me at last, however: 'When she's done with that,' he said, 'I'll have it off you for my lass.' I was so stunned I didn't answer, and Eric didn't say anything else.

I didn't feel critical of him then; I was very hurt by him and I didn't understand why he was still so coldly angry with me. The way he was behaving didn't seem to sit well with what I thought I knew of his character: he'd certainly been very good to me before I'd got pregnant and I'd believed he was genuinely fond of me.

As an unmarried mother in the 1950s, I'd have been naive not to have expected people to criticize and condemn me. I just hadn't expected it from my own brother – at least, not once the initial shock and disappointment in me had had time to wear off. Paradoxically, however, most of the people I lived and worked with were less censorial than I'd assumed they would be; whereas one of the only two people I'd hoped would stand by me – the other being my sister Mabel – was the harshest, cruellest critic of them all.

12

It was my twenty-first birthday in February 1952 and I decided to have a party. I invited some of the people I worked with as well as a few friends and my family – although not Eric. My mother invited Ernie Burns. My social life, such as it was, consisted primarily of going out for a drink sometimes in the evenings with my brother Harry, his wife Olive and some of their friends, and, very occasionally, if someone asked me, leaving Pat with my mother and Eddie and going dancing. I'd become friendly with a young South African man at work who was in England for just a few months and was missing his family and his girlfriend. So I invited him too.

There wasn't anyone who was 'interested' in me and I had no expectation of ever having a boyfriend. It was hardly likely that any young man would want to get involved with a girl who'd had someone else's baby, and certainly no one would want to marry her. It didn't upset me: it was just a fact of life that I accepted.

The party seemed to be going well until, having eaten the food I'd bought and prepared myself, my mother, Ernie Burns and all the other members of my family left and went to the pub, where they remained until it closed. Fortunately, my friends stayed with me at the house and although it turned out to be rather less of a party than I'd hoped, I pretended not to mind.

The following year was the year of the Queen's Coronation. On the day itself, 2 June 1953, a party was held at W. T. Flather for all its employees and their families. Now, that was a good party! There was a line of tables laden with a wonderful spread of food and a huge screen had been erected so that we could watch the ceremony taking place in London. I'd told some of the girls at work about my situation and I was sure it hadn't been long before everyone knew. So I was a bit nervous about taking Pat to the party. I needn't have been though. No one said anything unkind or treated Pat any differently from the way they treated all the other children who were there. She had a lovely time and I did too.

We didn't stay until the end of the party – Pat wasn't yet three years old and we left when she got tired. When we got home, the house was quiet and I assumed my mother had gone out. I'd turned on the tap in the kitchen and was starting to fill the kettle to make a cup of tea when I heard a noise. A few seconds later my mother walked down the stairs. Her face was red and her hair was all wisps and disarray. Realizing immediately what she'd been doing, I almost dropped the kettle on to the draining board and hurried Pat into the front room. I'd only just shut the door when I heard Ernie Burns' tread on the stairs and then the sound of the back door opening and closing.

It was horrible. In some respects, I wasn't in any position to judge, but I felt humiliated and ashamed on my mother's behalf. Clearly, she had no such qualms herself and when Pat and I went into the kitchen a few minutes later, she acted as though nothing had happened. And I did the same, because that's what I always did. In fact, that turned out to be the last time I was a reluctant witness to what had been going on between my mother and Ernie Burns for so many years.

A few months after I'd left George Cohen's, my friend Jean had left there too and had gone to work at Hatfield's steel mill. It was through her that I heard they were looking for a typist. The job paid a bit more money than I was earning, so I applied for it, and got it.

With the exception of the boss and some section managers, all the staff who worked there were women and, as usual, I was apprehensive about how they'd treat me. I needn't have worried: everyone was very nice to me and I was glad I'd made the move. Although I wasn't getting a great deal more money than I'd been earning before, every extra shilling helped in the uphill struggle to pay the bills and provide for Pat and myself.

One day, a girl at work I'd never actually spoken to got engaged and a couple of the other girls started going round the office collecting money to buy her a present.

'Everybody's got to put ten shillings in the kitty,' I was told.

I didn't have any money saved up – every penny I earned each week was accounted for – and if I had had money to spare, I'd have spent it on my child, not on a present for a woman I didn't even know. I felt cornered and horribly embarrassed as I told the girl, 'I'm very sorry, but I couldn't possibly put in as much as ten shillings. I could give you five.'

In reality, I couldn't afford even five shillings; I'd offered it because I didn't want to appear mean or unfriendly. I could have saved myself the trouble, and the money. Clearly unable to see my point of view, the women in the office 'sent me to Coventry'. It would have been bad enough if they'd simply stopped talking to me – which they did. Unfortunately though, that wasn't all they did.

My desk was in an alcove off the large main office and it faced the desk of another girl, who started giving a running commentary on everything I did. 'She's taking the cover off her typewriter,' she'd call out to the girls in the other office. 'Oh, now she's opening the drawer in her desk. She's taking out a pencil. She's put the pencil on the desk. She's turning round and putting her cardigan over the back of the chair.' It was spiteful and nasty and they kept it up for weeks.

Everything had been going so well. I had Pat living at home with me, she was happy and thriving, and I was earning enough, just, to provide for us both. And now I dreaded waking up in the mornings knowing that I had to go to work.

One morning, the small, toad-like man who was in charge of our section put his arm round my waist and tried to touch my breasts. It was the last straw. I was so worn down by what had been going on with the other girls that I could have burst into tears with the exhausting unhappiness of it all. Instead, something inside me seemed to snap. Turning my head slowly until I was looking directly into his face, I asked the man coldly, 'Do you think your wife would like to know that you did that?' He snatched his arm from round my waist as if he'd been burnt, and as I walked away from him, I'd already decided that the time had come for me to find another job.

A few days later, I started working at Plessey, an electronics and engineering company that was based in Ilford, in Essex, and had just opened a factory in Rotherham. I had a desk in a large office where I did the typing for a group of men (mostly) and women who were friendly and nice to me. It was a huge relief not to have to face all the unpleasantness I'd experienced every day in my last job; I felt as if I'd woken up from a nightmare.

Almost without my noticing it, the days had slipped by and Pat was four years old. Even allowing for the fact that I was her mother and I loved her more than I could ever have imagined it was possible to love anyone, she was a pretty little girl. She was bright and chatty too, and she made friends easily. Every single one of our neighbours would break into a smile and stop to talk to her whenever they saw her.

Perhaps the neighbour Pat liked best of all was a lady we called Auntie Flo. Whenever our backs were turned, Pat would slip out of the house to visit her. We always knew where she'd gone. Auntie Flo would sit patiently while Pat combed and brushed her hair, then she'd give her a drink and a biscuit and listen while Pat chirruped away about all the things cheerful, lively minded four-year-olds talk about.

It was never more than a minute or two before we realized Pat had gone: it was the quietness in the house that gave it away. And it was never long before we found her. On the very rare occasions when she wasn't at Auntie Flo's, she'd be with one of our other neighbours. All you had to do was listen for the sound of laughter through an open door and you'd know where she was.

One day, I couldn't find her in any of the usual places. I'd been to Auntie Flo's, who hadn't seen her, and I'd called at the houses of the other neighbours she'd be likely to be entertaining, but she wasn't with any of them either. By the fourth house I was beginning to feel uneasy. When I'd been to every house I'd ever known Pat to visit and I still couldn't find her, I knew for the first time in my life what it was like to feel absolute, heart-stopping panic.

Around the corner and up the hill from our house was Clifton Park, where Eddie and I used to play when we were children. Pat loved the park: perhaps she'd taken it into her head to go up there. I was already running up the road when I remembered that the two things she liked best about Clifton Park were feeding the ducks and paddling in the paddling pool. As I ran, I kept repeating silently in my head, 'Oh God, please don't let her have fallen into the pond.'

Despite my own brief experience in the blackout all those years earlier, I don't think it even crossed my mind that someone might hurt her. It was broad daylight and people who lived in communities like ours knew each other, if only by sight, and watched out for each other. Children often played outside, just like I'd done when I was a child – although I hadn't gone to the park alone when I was just four years old.

The abduction or deliberate harming of children by strangers was something you rarely heard about in those days, although it must have happened sometimes. I knew from what I'd been told by Annie and Mavis, the girls who'd shared my room at the unmarried mothers' home in Huddersfield, that some people did do terrible things to children. Fortunately, perhaps, I hadn't really been able to relate their experiences to real, everyday life; if I'd remembered them at that moment, when I was searching for Pat, I think I'd have been completely hysterical.

I was distraught by the time I reached the park. How could I have let this happen? When Pat wasn't at the pond or at the paddling pool, my mind did finally turn to the unspeakable alternatives. Pat was friendly with everyone; having always lived amongst people who knew her and were good to her, she had no reason to be afraid of any-one, which meant that she would have gone with someone if they'd asked her. I felt sick. Running back down the hill, I again prayed a silent prayer; this time, though, all I could say was 'Please'.

When I got home, my mother was beside herself too. In fact, she was more upset than I'd ever seen her about anything before.

I'd looked for Pat everywhere I could think of and I didn't know where else to look, so I went back to Auntie Flo's, just in case she'd turned up there while I'd been searching elsewhere. She hadn't. Auntie Flo looked pale and very anxious. 'I've been trying to think where she could be,' she told me. 'I've been racking my brains and I can't think of anywhere else. Did you go next door?'

The man who lived in the house next to Auntie Flo's was an elderly widower. Pat had never been to his house before, so I hadn't thought to knock on his door. And there she was, standing on a kitchen chair with her arms plunged up to the elbows in a bowl of soapy water, doing the old man's washing-up and having the time of her life.

I was too relieved to be cross with her; there'd have been no point anyway, because she wouldn't have understood why. I just wrapped my arms round her, almost squeezing all the breath out of her as I lifted her down from the chair, and then I explained why I'd burst into tears when I saw her.

'You must never, ever again go off on your own without telling me or Grandma or Uncle Eddie exactly where you're going,' I told her. 'Do you promise me?' She did promise, although I wasn't sure at the time if she'd really understood. I think she must have done, however, because she never did it again.

The poor man whose washing-up she'd been doing with considerably more enthusiasm than skill was very upset when he realized what had happened.

'I'm so sorry,' he kept saying. 'You must have been so worried about her. I assumed for some reason that Flo knew she was here. I'm so sorry.'

'It's all right,' I told him. And it *was* all right, because the only thing that mattered was that Pat was safe.

What happened that day was a salutary lesson for me. Perhaps it was all part of the learning curve for a young woman who'd never learned very much that was useful about parenting from her own mother and who was therefore having to make up motherhood as she went along.

Deciding to take the job at Plessey was one of those decisions you make in life that change everything. If I hadn't gone to work there, it's very likely that I wouldn't have met Roy. He told me later that he'd watched me walk through the factory and into the office on my first day and had made a life-changing decision of his own: he'd told himself that I was the woman for him.

Roy was very pleasant and friendly and I'd only been there for a few days when he asked me if I'd like to go to the cinema with him. One of the other men heard him ask and heard me say 'Yes', and when Roy had left the room, he told me, 'You want to be careful of him. He's got a fixation about his father; it's all he ever talks about: "My father this and my father that." It's an odd way for a man to carry on. Just be careful, that's all I'm saying.'

Of course I didn't take any notice. Being proud of your father didn't seem to be such a terrible thing to be guilty of: I would have liked to have been proud of my father, or even just to have had a legitimate father who I could acknowledge. I knew only too well what it was like to be the butt of people's malicious comments and although the warning was possibly well intentioned, it seemed unfair to say something unkind about a man who was apparently so nice.

Roy and I did go to the cinema; we had a very enjoyable evening, and afterwards he did talk about his parents. He told me that his father was Swiss and that he was the banqueting chef at the Savoy Hotel in London. It was clear that Roy was very proud of him, and that he had good reason to be so. What was also clear was that he loved his mother very much too. His obvious, unembarrassed affection for his parents seemed to me to be a good thing, and I was pleased when he asked me out again.

It was on our second date that I took a deep breath and told him, 'I've got a little girl.'

'Oh, that's nice,' he said. 'How old is she? I've got a daughter, too. She's at boarding school now, so unfortunately I don't get the chance to see her very often. It was a wartime marriage that didn't work out.' He laughed and shrugged his shoulders as he added, 'It's a story that's been told a thousand times. I divorced her mother when I came out of the RAF.' He asked me a few more questions about Pat and then he talked about something else, without giving any indication at all that he was perturbed by my single-mother status.

We started going out quite regularly after that and I began to grow fond of him. One evening, when he'd walked me home from the pictures and we were saying goodnight, my brother Eddie came sauntering down the road, nodded to us in discreet greeting and went into the house, closing the front door behind him. When I followed Eddie inside a few minutes later, he pulled a face and asked me, 'What on earth are you doing going out with an old man like that?'

'He *isn't* an old man,' I answered defensively. 'He's very nice, and he's kind.'

'Oh, he's kind is he?' Eddie laughed. 'Well, he might be kind but he's going bald! How old is he, for heaven's sake?'

'He's thirty-eight.' I turned away so that I wouldn't see the expression on my brother's face and, as I walked towards the stairs, I muttered again, 'He's very nice.'

Roy was one of several people who'd been sent up to Rotherham from London to help get Plessey's new factory up and running, and just before he was sent back again he said to me, 'I've told my parents all about you and they want me to invite you down to London for the weekend so they can meet you, and Pat too, of course.'

Ever since I'd realized that I was falling in love with Roy, I'd been concerned about whether he'd really be able to accept Pat. He was always kind to her, but she was another man's child and I couldn't imagine how a man in Roy's position would really feel about that. The invitation to London seemed to indicate that he was as accepting of it as he appeared to be and when the weekend came, Pat and I set off on her first-ever train journey feeling equally excited.

Roy met us at King's Cross station and took us on the underground to Seven Kings, where his parents lived. His mother and father were very welcoming and made a huge fuss of Pat, pronouncing her to be a 'charming little girl'. It was clear that we were both being given the 'once over', albeit in a very pleasant, polite way. When Roy's sister arrived a bit later with her little boy, who was about four years older than Pat, she was kind and friendly too. I could see why he was so attached to his family.

Watching Roy interacting with his parents, it quickly

became obvious that he was very much in awe of his father. Oscar Muller was a large man who spoke several languages, including excellent English, albeit with a thick Swiss accent. He was clearly a talented chef too: as well as winning many awards for the dishes he'd created, he'd cooked for some famous people. He had a box full of memories, including a cheque Bob Hope had given him, which he'd never banked, and a note from Winston Churchill that said something like 'Thank you for making my stomach happy, but you can't cook potatoes properly!' *I*'d have been proud of him if he'd been *my* father.

Roy's daughter was away at boarding school, so we didn't see her when we were in London. Roy obviously didn't like talking about her, which I assumed was because he missed her and because he didn't want to think about what had happened between him and her mother.

Pat and I had a wonderful weekend in London with Roy and his family and our visit seemed to strengthen the bonds that had already formed between Roy and me. He came up to Rotherham a couple of weekends later and then, after we'd known each other for about three months, he asked me to marry him.

Although I was thrilled to be asked, my first reaction was, 'What about Pat?'

'What *about* Pat?' he said. 'She's part of you, so I love her too. Pat's no problem. In fact, I've thought about this very carefully and there aren't any problems at all.'

So I said 'Yes' and Roy gave me a beautiful solitaire diamond engagement ring.

When I told my family and showed them the ring, their

relief was almost palpable: not only was someone prepared to marry me, a fallen woman; they were also willing to accept Pat, who was another man's child.

I could barely believe it either. I hadn't expected ever to get married and now, suddenly, the future looked rosier than I had ever imagined it could possibly be.

13

When we talked about where we were going to be married, Roy said, 'It's going to be difficult. If we do it in Rother-ham, all my family will have to travel up from London. If we get married in London, all your family will have to travel down there. I'll give it some thought and see if I can come up with a solution.' And, very shortly afterwards, he did.

My younger brother Eddie and his fiancée, Iris, had set the day for their wedding on Saturday 5 February 1955. Roy had been invited, of course, and when he came up on the train to Rotherham on the Friday evening, he told me, 'It's all fixed. We're getting married tomorrow morning. We'll make some excuse, nip out to the register office and be back in time for Eddie and Iris's wedding. I've booked a room at a hotel for tomorrow night. We can't tell any-one, mind. We don't want to steal the thunder from Eddie and Iris. It's their big day and they've been planning it for ages.'

A secret wedding! It sounded very romantic.

The next morning, while everyone was getting ready, Roy and I slipped out of the house and, in the presence of two cheerful, friendly strangers who acted as our wit-nesses, I became Mrs Roy Muller. After having a quick celebratory drink at a hotel, I took the wedding ring off my finger and we went back to join Eddie and Iris and their guests.

People in the 1950s didn't have the huge, expensive weddings that have become the norm today, and after the ceremony we went back to Iris's parents' house. While we were there, someone said something unkind to Olive, my brother Harry's wife, and she was very upset.

'Don't take any notice,' I whispered to her. 'It's just the drink talking. Please, Olive, don't cry. Look, come outside with me and I'll tell you something that'll cheer you up.'

We slid our arms into our coats and when we were standing together outside the back door, I told her, 'I'm going to let you into a secret. No one else knows anything about it, so you must promise not to tell anyone.'

Olive dabbed at her eyes with a damp handkerchief and asked, 'What? What is it? Is it a good secret?'

'Yes,' I laughed. 'It's a very good secret – for me, at least. Roy and I were married this morning.'

'That's wonderful!' Olive flung her arms round me. 'Oh, Sheila, I'm so happy for you, and for Pat too. It's obvious Roy loves you, and he really does seem to be fond of Pat.'

'But don't forget,' I said, 'it's a secret so you mustn't breathe a word about it to anyone. Promise?'

'Yes, I promise!' Olive hugged me again, her tears already forgotten.

So that Roy and I could stay that night in the hotel room he'd booked, I had to tell my mother too, so that she'd look after Pat. Although she was very surprised at the news, she didn't say very much, except that she hadn't really believed I would ever get married.

Roy had to go back to his job in London on the Sunday, and of course I had to stay in Rotherham and go to mine. There were many plans and decisions that had to be made, including where we were going to live. We decided to get a mortgage and buy a place of our own and I agreed with Roy that it would be nice to live near his family. His mother and sister began scouring the area around Seven Kings for suitable properties, but they couldn't find anything we could afford and after a while they extended their search area.

I was at work one day when Roy phoned me. 'We've found somewhere!' he announced triumphantly. 'I knew we would if we looked hard enough. It's a brand new bungalow, one of several that are still being built.' The line crackled and I missed part of what he said next. When I could hear him again, he was saying, '. . . and we can move in as soon as it's finished, which will be within the next few weeks. You'll really like it, Sheila. I know you will. It's Billy –' the line crackled again – '. . . in Essex.'

'Billy Who's in Essex?' I asked him, but the phone was dead.

When I told the men in the office what Roy had said and that he'd got cut off in the middle of telling me about someone in Essex called Billy, they roared with laughter.

'Billericay,' one of them told me. 'That's what he was saying. It's a small town, east of London, in the middle of nowhere really. You know, one of those places you can't see the point of.' Noticing the look of dismay on my face, he laughed again and added quickly, 'I'm sure it's very nice though, and a brand new bungalow sounds wonderful.'

It turned out that Roy's mother, Lil, had lived in Billericay as a girl and many of her relatives were still there. It was from there that she'd gone to work as a receptionist at the Savoy Hotel during the First World War and had met Roy's father, who'd left Switzerland after finishing his training as a chef and had arrived in London just before war broke out. Oscar and Lil had lived in Billericay after they were married and it was where Roy himself had been born.

Shortly after Roy's phone call, Pat and I went down to London again for the weekend to have a look at the house Roy had found. After living for as long as I could remember in a small terraced house with an outside toilet, no bathroom and no plumbed hot water, the bungalow seemed like a palace. It had every conceivable luxury. As well as two bedrooms, there was a large sitting room, a well-equipped kitchen with a gas cooker and hot water 'on tap', a bathroom, also with a hot-water tap, and a separate, *inside*, toilet.

When I returned to Rotherham after the weekend, I gave in my notice at work. A few days later, Pat and I were on the train again, this time with one-way tickets to our new life as a family.

Roy worked at Plessey's in Seven Kings, travelling to work by bus every day from the house in Billericay. Pat had taken the move in her stride, as she did most things, and she seemed to be as happy in our new home as I was.

While Roy was at work, we were never short of things to do: we'd go on bus rides, sometimes to explore the area and sometimes just for the fun of it; and we'd work side by side in our little garden.

The garden was full of what seemed to be an infinite and inexhaustible supply of old bricks and rubble, which kept coming to the surface however deeply I dug. It was exhausting work, but I was determined that I was going to transform it from builder's tip into something that warranted the name of garden.

One day, I had a brilliant idea: we didn't have a coal bunker and it occurred to me that I could solve two problems at once by building one using all the bricks I'd been digging out of the earth and piling up in a corner. There were builders working on some other bungalows that were still being built around ours and when I told one of them what I was planning to do, he gave me a small bag of cement.

I worked on that coal bunker for hours and when I finally stepped back, stretched my aching limbs and surveyed the finished job, I couldn't wait to show it to Roy. When he got home from work later that day, I almost dragged him out into the garden and, with a dramatic sweep of my hand, revealed to him the fruits of my extensive labours.

His reaction wasn't quite what I'd anticipated and I was upset when he burst into laughter.

'Well, I can't see what's so funny,' I told him huffily. 'I've been working hard all day and ... Will you *please* stop laughing!'

'I'm sorry,' he said at last. 'It *was* a brilliant idea, and I can see that you've put a lot of thought and effort into it.' He paused and cleared his throat. 'Err . . . Have you ever noticed how rows of bricks are always staggered rather than being one on top of the other? There's a reason for that: if you pile them up as you've done, it takes just one push to send the whole lot crashing to the ground.'

As he said the last word, he placed the open palm of his hand against one wall of my magnificent coal bunker and pushed and the whole thing collapsed like a pack of cards, exactly as he'd said it would. I had to laugh too, and I consoled myself with the thought that most bricklayers probably couldn't type.

Fortunately, I had more success with the plant-related side of gardening. Once I'd dug the soil and cleared as many of the bricks and as much of the debris as I could, I bought some plants at one of the many nurseries in the area, put them in the soil, watered them and developed a love of gardening that remained with me and gave me many hours of pleasure for years to come.

While we were living in Billericay, my mother came to stay for what proved to be an awkward, uncomfortable few days – I don't know why I'd imagined it might be any other way. There was only one pub near where we lived and as Roy and I couldn't afford to take her there every night, she soon became bored and restless. And, when my mother wasn't happy, she could see no possible reason for keeping her dissatisfaction to herself.

During the visit she confided in me one day, when

Roy was at work, that her relationship with Ernie Burns had finally ended. It wasn't something I really wanted to know or to talk about. It had been the cause of huge embarrassment to me throughout my entire childhood, an embarrassment I'd learned to live with by ignoring it and pretending it wasn't happening.

'His wife died at last,' my mother told me, 'and when I asked him to marry me, like he'd always promised he'd do if she wasn't around, he said he wouldn't. After me waiting all these years!'

I tried to suppress an involuntary shudder. It's a horrible feeling to have about your own mother, but in that moment I felt that I wanted to draw away from her, physically as well as mentally, so that I didn't become contaminated by her complete and utter selfish unpleasantness.

'I told John to go and see him,' she continued. 'I told him to go and tell Ernie that now he could marry me, he should, after all this time.'

I felt sick: I couldn't even begin to imagine how my brother John, who was the gentlest, kindest man I'd ever known, must have felt about her request.

'And do you know what John said?' Her voice rose upwards on a wave of indignant outrage. 'He said he wouldn't do it! Can you imagine that? Can you think of one reason why our John would be like that? I can't. I thought better of him.'

I didn't ever argue with my mother: I'd long ago learned that it was a futile exercise and one from which I always came off worse. This time, though, from somewhere deep inside me, I found the courage to speak out: 'I can completely understand why John said no. You've put Ernie Burns before all of us throughout all our lives. He's always come first, before your own children. Nothing mattered to you as much as he did. He had to be thought of in everything. Didn't you know that none of us liked him? So no, I'm not surprised John didn't want to go and talk to him. Why should he?'

While I was talking, my mother was looking at me as if I was speaking a foreign language she didn't understand. When I stopped to draw breath, she glared at me and then muttered again, as if I hadn't said anything at all, 'Yes, well, I was surprised at our John.'

I did agree with her, silently, on one point though: it was horrible of Ernie Burns to use her for sex for all those years, encouraging her to believe that one day he'd leave his wife and marry her, when he obviously had never had any intention of doing any such thing. She paid dearly, one way and another, for all those years when she put him first; all they cost *him* was the price of a few glasses of Guinness. He wasn't a nice man by any standard, and I wished he wasn't my father or, at the very least, that I didn't know he was.

It was my mother-in-law who eventually came to our rescue by inviting my mother to stay with her for a couple of days. I imagine the sound of my sighs of gratitude and relief must have travelled ahead of her all the way from Billericay to Seven Kings. What I can't imagine is what Roy's parents must have made of her: they were far too polite ever to say.

*

We'd been living in the bungalow for just a few months when Roy came home from work one day and told me he'd had a row with his boss and had handed in his notice. I wasn't working and I wondered how we were going to manage, particularly as we had a mortgage to pay, although I didn't say anything at the time about my concerns.

I hadn't met any of Roy's friends, so I didn't know Joe and Betty, the couple who invited us to London to spend a week with them shortly after Roy gave up his job. It turned out that their invitation had an ulterior motive, as they'd recently taken over as tenants of a pub in the East End and needed help while their regular cleaners and bar staff were on holiday.

I hadn't ever worked behind a bar before and I was very nervous that first lunchtime when a group of young men came in from the brewery offices round the corner. The prices of only some of the drinks were written down; I had to try to remember the rest of them and keep a tally in my head of all the drinks I was dispensing so that I asked for the right amount of money and gave people the right change. Fortunately, I was good at mental arithmetic.

I'd just served my first customer, who'd also ordered drinks for a couple of his friends, and had rung up the total cost on the old-fashioned till – which wasn't old-fashioned at the time, of course – when the drawer shot open and hit me in the bosom. There were a lot of young men standing around the bar and they all roared with laughter. I was so embarrassed I just wanted the floor under my feet to collapse into the cellar below, taking me with it.

When I'd recovered my composure, I made sure I always stood to one side of the till and reached across to press its keys. The quizzical looks I got from some people were far less embarrassing than it would have been to have repeated what had happened the first time. After that, things seemed to be going quite well, until Betty asked me to make some sandwiches.

The pub was very busy and I was glad to escape into the kitchen for a while and have a break from the noisy, cigarette-smoke-filled bar. Betty had given me very precise instructions about the fillings to put in the sandwiches and after I'd made them, I cut each one into four neat squares, arranged them carefully on a plate and carried them out of the kitchen to the bar, feeling pretty pleased with myself.

When Betty saw me, she glanced down at the plate in my hands and said, 'Oh, Sheila! You shouldn't have cut them like that! Don't you know that sandwiches should *always* be cut on the diagonal?'

I hadn't known; but judging from the shocked tone of her voice, I'd just driven a coach and horses through the north–south divide.

'I'm sorry,' I told her, actually feeling more embarrassed than sorry. 'I'm afraid I didn't know.'

'Well, never mind now,' she said, in what seemed to me to be an unnecessarily patronizing tone of voice. 'Just don't do them like that again, will you?' Which I thought was a bit rich, considering how hard I'd been working and the fact that we'd only been invited to stay so that she and her husband would have a couple of unpaid labourers for the week, while Pat was more or less left to amuse herself – which, fortunately, she did very well, bless her.

At the end of the week, I think Joe gave Roy ten pounds. It didn't really repay us for all the work we'd done, although what he did for Roy more than made up for it.

'Quite a few of the bosses from Mann Crossman, the brewery that owns this pub, come in here at lunchtime,' Joe had told Roy at the beginning of the week. 'I'll have a word with them, if you'd like me to, and see if there's any possibility of a job for you.'

A couple of days later, word had come back to Roy that although he didn't have the experience necessary to manage a pub, the brewery was looking for a couple to run an off-licence. If Roy was interested, all he had to do was go and see them.

It was September when we sold the bungalow in Billericay and went to live in a large flat above an off-licence on the corner of Hamstel Road in Southend-on-Sea. As well as being paid a salary, we had rent-free accommodation: we were back on our feet and things were looking up. As far as working in an off-licence was concerned, Roy and I were at the bottom of another learning curve. It wasn't long, though, before I was lifting and stacking crates of beer as if I'd been doing it all my life.

Pat was five and shortly after we moved she started school for the first time. It was just before that, however, when we were still settling in to our new life, that Joe and Betty came down from London to visit us on our day off and we all went out to lunch. We ordered fish and chips for Pat and when the plate was put down in front of her, it was piled so high with food that most adults couldn't have eaten it all, let alone a little girl.

For some reason I couldn't understand, Roy insisted she must eat every last mouthful. I knew he had a bee in his bonnet about not wasting food, but this wasn't a case of being wasteful: Pat hadn't asked for a huge plateful of fish and chips. In fact, I don't think she'd even been asked what she wanted to eat. Nevertheless, Roy started going on at her about the millions of people in Africa who were starving and who'd give their right arm for even a fraction of the food that was on her plate, none of which was relevant or fair in the circumstances.

At first I thought he was joking, but there was no humour in his voice when he said to Pat, 'You will not leave this table until you have eaten every last mouthful. Don't make me have to tell you again: *eat* it.'

I was distressed because Pat was upset and I was embarrassed because Roy was making a scene in front of Joe and Betty – and everyone else in the café. I tried to explain to him, 'I don't think she *can* eat it, Roy. There's simply too much for her.' When Betty came to her defence too, Roy raised his hand as if to deflect the sound of our voices and told Pat again, 'You will eat *all* of it.'

I could see that Pat desperately wanted to do as Roy told her and that she didn't understand what she'd done wrong. She simply couldn't eat it all though, and eventually Roy had no choice other than to allow her to leave some of it. He refused to speak to her, or to me, for the rest of the afternoon, and the whole day was ruined for everyone.

I've always hated any type of scene or argument. Confrontations like that make my stomach churn and the palms of my hands sweat. So I let the incident pass without saying anything about what had happened, which was a very bad mistake.

It wasn't long after that day with Joe and Betty when I asked Roy for his daughter's address.

'Why? Why do you want it?' he snapped at me.

Taken aback by his reaction, I could hear the placating tone in my voice as I said, 'It's her birthday next week, isn't it? I've bought a card and a present for us to send to her.'

Even if I'd known that Roy hadn't ever sent his daughter anything for her birthday or for Christmas since he and her mother had separated, I still don't think I'd have understood why, for the first time since I'd known him, he seemed to lose his temper completely and shouted at me.

It was a few days later when he finally told me the truth about the daughter he never saw.

'My mother's cross with me,' he said, apropos of nothing one day. 'She says that if I don't tell you about Valerie, she will. The fact is that I don't pay for her to go to a private boarding school. She lives with her mother.'

I didn't understand why he'd lied, but I didn't make a song and dance about it. I loved him and trusted him, so I assumed he'd had his reasons and put it out of my mind. It was another bad mistake.

14

Pat had started school and Roy and I had been married for about eight months when something far worse happened. Pat was playing on the floor and, for some reason I can't now remember, she had a tea towel, which Roy trod on. I still want to believe that he didn't do it on purpose and that he hadn't realized her hand was underneath it. She yelped and started to cry, and there was no mistaking the nastiness in his voice as he told her, 'Well, it serves you right. You know I don't like you anyway.'

When I stared at him in astonishment, I don't think he even noticed me. For a moment I forgot to breathe and then I felt sick. How could anyone say such a terrible thing to a child? Even more importantly, how could Roy have said something like that to a sweet, lovely little girl like Pat – *my* little girl? I was so completely stunned and devastated by it that, to my eternal shame, I didn't say anything. I didn't ever forgive him though: in fact, if he were to stand in front of me today and say, 'I'm sorry. Can you forgive me?' I'd have to tell him, 'No.'

That night, I wrote a letter to my mother asking if I could send Pat back to Rotherham to live with her. I don't remember what I gave as the reason for what must have seemed like a strange request; I certainly didn't tell the truth about what had happened. I was very relieved when

I received a letter a few days later in which my mother said, 'Yes, of course Pat can come here. I'd love to have her.' It was the answer I'd been hoping for. My mother didn't love me, but I was thankful that she was fond of Pat.

I tried to make light of it when I told Roy what I was planning to do. He didn't react at all until I'd finished my awkward explanation; then he shrugged and said casually, 'Fine. But if she goes, you go with her.'

I felt as though I'd been playing a game and, without any warning, someone had changed the rules so that I no longer understood what I was supposed to do. Roy had always been nice to Pat. The fish-and-chip incident had been the first indication there'd ever been that he was irritated by her in any way or felt any animosity towards her. I'd thought he really did care for her, which meant that the way he'd spoken to her and what he was saying to me now made no sense. I was deeply hurt: I loved Roy and, quite apart from not wanting to leave him, I wasn't prepared to give up on our marriage and go crawling back to Rotherham with my tail between my legs.

A couple of days later, I wrote to my mother again and told her, 'It's all right. Pat's going to stay here. It's all blown over.'

Looking back on it now, I suppose Roy was afraid of what my family, and his, would think of him if I had to send my child to live with my mother. It would have looked so bad for him. And I suppose he knew I wouldn't leave him. I can't think of any other reason why he made that conditional statement.

For the next few weeks, things were better and eventually

I put the whole thing to the back of my mind and hoped that Pat would forget it had ever happened. Roy wasn't unkind to her again in the way he'd been the time when he stepped on her fingers and told her he didn't like her, but he did seem to have developed resentment towards her that he sometimes didn't – or couldn't – hide. I couldn't think of any reason why he'd suddenly become hostile towards her, or why he was sometimes short-tempered and critical of her. All I could do was try to keep her out of his way as much as possible so that she didn't 'annoy' him. And then I had an idea.

One evening, when we were sitting together in the living room of the flat above the off-licence, I asked him, 'Wouldn't it be nice if you had a son?'

'Hmm, not really,' he answered, glancing up at me briefly from the newspaper he was reading. 'For a start, you may be only twenty-five, but I'm forty years old, so I'd be sixty when he was twenty. Anyway, we can't afford another mouth to feed.'

Despite his emphatic response, I didn't give up. In fact, I became convinced that if he had a son of his own – and, for some reason, I was certain that it *would* be a son and not a daughter – he'd feel differently about everything, including Pat.

Eventually I won him over, and it turned out that I was right about it being a son: Peter was born in October 1957, weighing ten pounds four ounces. This time I gave birth at home, with the help of a lovely midwife. Almost everything about Peter's birth was as different as it could possibly have been from Pat's, except for one thing: when he was placed in my arms for the first time, I had exactly the same instant, overwhelmingly powerful feeling of love for him that I'd had seven years earlier for Pat.

Pat was thrilled to bits to have a baby brother and she loved him, too, from the moment she first set eyes on him. She couldn't wait to hold him. I could see Roy was agitated: he kept making nervous darting movements towards her, as if he wanted to snatch the baby away and stop her touching her little brother. Trying to reassure them both, I told Pat, 'It's all right. You sit down and I'll show you how to hold him. You have to do it very carefully.' When I laid the baby in her arms, the look of intense concentration and unqualified pride on her face brought tears to my eyes.

I'd been right about something else as well: Roy was over the moon to have a son. He absolutely adored Peter from the moment he was born and for the rest of his life. What I'd been disastrously wrong about, however, was how Peter's birth would affect Roy's feelings towards Pat. The fact that he was totally besotted with his son meant that he became even more indifferent to her than he'd been before, and the contrast between the way he treated her and the way he treated Peter was as obvious as it was hurtful.

He would occasionally do something nice for Pat. For example, he always cut and filed her fingernails – he used to tell her, 'If you look after them, they'll grow into a nice shape' – and he encouraged her to read. Roy loved reading and he'd often bring books home from the library for Pat, including some by an author called Jeffery Farnol, which were very popular at the time. However, it was all some-how done at arm's length, with a sort of detachment, and he was never effusive or affectionate towards her.

I used to wonder why he seemed to resent her and the only explanation I could ever think of was that she was living proof of my 'affair' with another man. It certainly didn't seem to be for any reason directly related to Pat herself, or to anything she ever did, because she was a really lovely child.

Before I'd met and married Roy, I'd been contacted, out of the blue, by Pat's father. He'd gone back to his wife at some point after I'd told him I was pregnant, and in the letter he wrote to me he said he'd decided to go back into the RAF.

'I'm sure you know that you can contact the RAF and ask for the maintenance payments to be deducted from my pay,' he wrote. 'I'm asking you not to do that, because if you do, it will eventually get all round the base and then my wife will find out. So, please, don't do it.'

I don't know why he thought I'd be sympathetic to his plight: 'people finding out' had been a very real cause of anxiety for me for a long time, both before and after Pat was born.

He'd failed persistently and repeatedly to send even the very small amount of money he'd been ordered to pay towards Pat's 'maintenance'. I'd had to chase him time after time to try to get for her what she was entitled to, usually without much success. I'd accepted that that was the way things were and the way they were going to be for the foreseeable future. But I was annoyed by his self-serving letter and his assumption that I'd feel sorry for him and would want to help shield him from the consequences of his own actions.

I wrote to the address he'd given me and told him 'I'll think about it'. I didn't do anything about it until later though, after I'd married, when I finally decided, 'No, blow you. At least if the money's being stopped from your wages, I'll be sure of getting it at last.'

I didn't do it because I wanted to make his life difficult. I felt that if he was paying the money he was supposed to be paying, Roy would have less reason to be resentful about Pat, and now that he'd given me the information I needed to secure regular payments, it was an opportunity I would have been foolish to pass up.

I did start to receive regular payments a little while after that and then one day, a few weeks after Peter was born, I had a letter from the court. Apparently, what Pat's father had been so afraid of had happened and his wife had found out that he had a daughter. Her reaction hadn't been what he'd expected, however, and according to the letter, after they'd discussed 'the matter', they'd decided they'd like to adopt Pat. The court was writing to me to pass on their 'offer' and could I please write back, care of the address above, to let them know how I felt about it.

I sat down almost immediately to do exactly that, although, fortunately for all concerned, I managed to control my indignant fury and instead of asking them how they had the nerve to make such a request, I said, 'Pat has a baby brother and she's living in a nice family home. There is absolutely no chance at all of her ever going to live with anyone else. And, by the way, she is not a parcel to be passed from hand to hand.' I thought it was very restrained, given the circumstances.

Pat's father had kept her existence a secret from his wife and, as far as I knew, from everyone else for all those years. He hadn't offered to help me in any way when I was pregnant and he had never tried to do anything to help Pat. Now that his secret was out, he and his wife thought, for reasons best known to themselves, that it might be nice to have a ready-grown seven-year-old daughter about whom they knew absolutely nothing. *And* they thought I would give her up, just like that. It was clear from the very fact that they'd made the suggestion that they didn't have any understanding at all of what it means to love a child.

Roy, on the other hand, really did love his son. When Peter was a baby, he slept in a cot in our bedroom, next to my side of the bed, and whenever he woke up and cried in the night, Roy would leap out of bed and pick him up before I'd even opened my eyes.

When Peter was older, Roy always put him to bed, a process that involved playing rough-and-tumble games with him every night until he was so over-excited he couldn't sleep. Pat would watch for a while, wide-eyed and smiling, as Peter rolled around on the floor, shrieking with laughter. And when she tried to join in with their games, Roy would put his hand out to block her or turn his back on her to stop her. The look of hurt confusion on her face was unbearable and I hated the fact that I couldn't do anything about it. The relationship Roy developed with

Peter was exclusive and, as far as Roy was concerned, I was outside it too.

Despite his genuine love for his son, it wasn't only with Pat that Roy sometimes lost his temper. Peter was just two years old the first time his father turned his anger on him. We'd gone up to stay with my mother in Rotherham and after I'd got Peter ready to go out to visit one of my brothers and his family, I went upstairs. A few minutes later, I heard Peter screaming. When I ran down the stairs and into the kitchen/living room, he was crouching in a corner behind the open door and Roy was shouting at him and hitting him – a two-year-old child!

'Whatever are you doing to him?' I shrieked at Roy. 'What's the matter? What's he done?'

With one hand raised and the fingers of the other gripping Peter's little arm, Roy turned his head, looked at me coldly, and said, 'He went out into the yard and got dirt on his clothes.' In other circumstances, it might have sounded like a joke: why would anyone beat a small child for getting dirt on his clothes? It didn't make any sense.

Although Roy sometimes appeared to lose control of his temper with the children, he didn't ever shout at me or hit me. Perhaps it was simply because he thought I'd fight back in a way a child can't do. I suppose, too, that I'd learned to watch for any sign that his mood might be changing and not to do anything that annoyed him. Until the day he hit Peter, I'd thought it was only Pat I had to try to keep out of Roy's way when he was in one of his tempers. It's a horrible feeling, like being punched in the stomach, when you realize that the person you've married isn't the person you thought they were at all.

When Peter was four and Pat was almost eleven, we moved from the flat above the off-licence in Southend-on-Sea. Roy had been having trouble with his knee for some time. It was causing him a great deal of pain and he eventually went to the doctor. When an X-ray proved inconclusive, it was decided that he should have exploratory surgery. His leg was cut open behind the knee, but they still couldn't find out what was wrong and after the operation he couldn't stand for long periods of time, which meant that working in the off-licence was no longer a viable proposition. Fortunately, he was offered a job in the offices at Mann Crossman's brewery in the East End of London.

Living in London was a new experience for me, some aspects of which were good and some not so good. Roy's new job didn't pay a very good salary, but although it was difficult for us to make ends meet financially, we were provided with a two-floor flat above a pub in Whitechapel that had been closed and turned into offices for the brewery's advertising section. The flat was just round the corner from the Blind Beggar pub on Whitechapel Road, where, a few years later in 1966, the East End gangster Ronnie Kray shot and murdered a rival gang member. (On a more positive note, it was outside the Blind Beggar pub that William Booth, the founder of the Salvation Army, preached his first sermon.)

Pat went to a good local school, where she settled in

well. She hadn't been going there for very long, however, when she came home one day feeling ill and it turned out that she'd caught chickenpox. From the way Roy behaved, you'd have thought she'd been afflicted by a particularly virulent form of bubonic plague. Without showing any signs of sympathy for Pat at all, he became fixated on preventing Peter from catching chickenpox from her.

Using various bits of furniture, including the fireguard, he constructed a barricade around the chair she sat on and kept reminding her – and me – that she must have 'no physical contact whatsoever with Peter'. Pat did try to do what Roy told her, but Peter was only four years old and when Pat offered him a sweet – without thinking that giving it to him would involve 'physical contact' – he clambered on to the barricade, reached out his hand, took it and put it into his mouth before anyone could stop him.

Roy went absolutely crazy. He shouted and screamed at Pat and then, when both children were thoroughly upset and sobbing, he slammed out of the room and refused to speak to her, or to me, for days. I'm still angry with myself for not standing up to him. When he ranted and shouted at Pat – on that occasion and on others too – I should have said, 'Don't be ridiculous! Don't talk to her like that.' But I was a coward, a lot of the time. There'd often be no sign at all that Roy was getting angry and when his rage suddenly erupted, my stomach would churn and I'd feel like a frightened little girl, bemused and too afraid to say anything. And I think he'd worked out what he could get away with.

There *were* periods when everything was calm and life

seemed to be going along nicely. The problem was that you never knew how long those periods were going to last, or what might trigger Roy's anger or days of wordless, soul-destroying sulking. Living under the sword of Damocles like that meant that the better times counted for nothing in the end, because I was always waiting and watching for anything that might set Roy off, and I could never relax.

The flat in London was on a main road, on the opposite side of which was a garage with a large metal door that was used by a couple and their two sons who had a greengrocery business. The family used to park their trucks there every night, and on wet days the mother would arrive early in the morning and set up her stall under shelter, just inside the garage. It was a successful business, judging by the brisk trade she did even on wet days, and it was obvious that the whole family worked very hard.

One day when it was raining and a cold wind was blowing discarded bits of paper down the road, I looked out of the window, saw the woman standing by her stall and thought, 'I'll take her a cup of tea.' She was very grateful for it, and when I did the same thing again a few days later, I offered to stay and serve on her stall while she drank it. When she handed me the empty cup, she said, 'You were good. Would you like a job working on the stall?'

'Oh, no, I don't think so, thank you,' I told her. But it set me thinking, and not long afterwards I asked Roy if it would be all right with him if I started looking for work. We needed the money I could earn, and he agreed.

Apart from helping Roy in the off-licence, I'd only ever

previously worked as an office clerk and then a typist. However, I *had* passed my School Certificate and it seemed foolish not to put it to good use and try to get a better-paid job. I asked a woman I'd made friends with, who ran a local shop and had a little boy of Peter's age, if she'd look after Peter so that I could work full time, and a few days later, I started work as a cashier at the Westminster Bank in Moorgate. I was earning a good salary and I loved the job from the very first day.

Pat was happy at school, Peter was happy spending weekdays with his little friend, Roy had a job and we were living in a flat for which we didn't have to pay much rent: everything was working out well. And then I made a stupid mistake.

One day, a customer came into the bank and after chatting to me for a few moments, he asked me to have lunch with him. I said 'no', of course, and I was laughing as I told Roy what had happened. By the time I'd realized that Roy wasn't smiling and I shouldn't have told him, it was too late.

He didn't speak to me again that evening, and the next morning he told me he'd phoned my boss at the bank to let him know that I was quitting my job, with immediate effect, and wouldn't be going in to work there again. I felt humiliated, embarrassed and very disappointed, but there was nothing I could do about it.

Not long after my abrupt 'resignation' from the bank, Roy told me he wanted to move again. Apparently, he'd read in a newspaper that Basildon Council was looking for rent collectors, so he'd applied for a job and got it. I didn't argue about that move, or about any of the others we made over the next few years. They were hard for the children though, particularly for Pat, who didn't tell me until many years later how much she always dreaded having to start at a new school, trying to fit in and make new friends.

While we were living in Basildon, I suffered from some health problems that culminated in my having to have major surgery. Roy's sister very kindly offered to look after Pat and Peter and I was admitted to a hospital in Southend-on-Sea. During the two or three weeks I was there, Roy came to visit me once. The bus fare from Basildon was an expense we couldn't afford, he told me. And as I didn't have money to send him, the way I'd sent it to my mother when I was in the unmarried mothers' home in Huddersfield, he didn't come again.

I'd only just come out of hospital when Roy said, 'I don't like tramping the streets collecting rents. I've decided to go back to running an off-licence.' He didn't ask my opinion: he'd already made up his mind, gone for an interview and accepted a job in Chessington. A couple of days later, he hired a car, invited his parents to go with us, and we drove to Chessington to have a look at our new home.

I sat in the back of the car with Lil, Roy's mother, and Pat, with Peter on my knee. I was still sore after the operation and it was an uncomfortable journey, although I knew better than to complain. Whenever Roy hired a car to go anywhere, his parents always came with us. Despite the proud, admiring way he talked about his father, it was his mother he really adored, and she adored him too.

Their close relationship was the cause of some problems between Roy and his father, who felt — with some justification, I think — that his son was more important to his wife than he was.

I wasn't sure *who* was important to Roy by that time: I knew he loved Peter and I think I still believed he loved me. What was even less certain, however, was how I felt about him.

We'd barely had time to unpack our things at the flat in Chessington before Roy decided that the off-licence wasn't the right one for 'us'. It was on a corner where a group of teenagers used to gather in the evenings. I didn't ever see them doing anything except hanging around smoking cigarettes, talking and joking with each other, as teenagers do. But Roy found their presence unnerving.

At first, he just said he was worried that they might get up to mischief, and then he told me he was going to look for another shop, somewhere else, away from street corners where teenagers hung out. Again, I wasn't being asked for my opinion, and when Roy told me he'd found a *much* better place in Epsom, one of a family-run group of off-licences where the hours were better and the flat above it was *huge*, I knew that our next move had already been decided.

There was just one problem: it turned out that Roy had been secretly drinking from the stock at the shop in Chessington without paying for it, and a substantial sum of money had to be put in the till before anyone found out. I discovered what he'd been doing one day when I went into the stockroom at the back of the shop.

Roy was busy serving customers, and I decided to help out by starting to sort through the empty bottles. In those days, you'd be given a few pennies when you returned bottles to the shops where you'd bought them, and we used to put the empties in a large wooden trolley until we had time to sort them into crates to be picked up by the suppliers. I'd taken a few bottles off the trolley when I noticed some miniature vodka bottles underneath them. As I cleared more of the full-sized bottles away, I could see that the whole of the bottom of the trolley was covered with empty miniatures.

I just stood there for a few minutes, looking at all these bottles and trying to think of an explanation as to how they'd got there. When I told Roy what I'd found, he was like a little boy being confronted by the evidence of something naughty he'd done. He didn't shout and lose his temper as he'd normally do if he felt he was being questioned about something. He didn't even raise his voice.

'I started drinking them to give myself Dutch courage,' he told me. 'In case those boys decided to make trouble.'

'What boys?' I asked him, now totally bemused.

'You know,' he said, 'the boys who hang around outside. I just had one or two bottles to begin with, and then somehow it got a bit out of hand.'

I suppose it was an explanation of sorts, although I still didn't really understand. He hadn't been paying for what he was drinking, so what had he thought was going to happen when the brewery found out? In a relatively short period of time, he'd drunk fifty pounds' worth of vodka, which was a great deal of money at that time. Quite apart from the moral obligation of paying it back, the fact that we were going to leave the off-licence meant that there'd be an audit and the discrepancy in the accounts would be glaringly obvious. There was no alternative: the money had to be paid back before the brewery became aware it was missing.

Roy was contrite and promised it wouldn't ever happen again and I didn't really question him any further about why he'd done it – I didn't want him to feel worse than he already did. I just went to the bank and took out a loan for fifty pounds.

When we moved to Epsom, Pat started at yet another new school. She hadn't been there very long, however, when she took her eleven-plus exam, passed it and got a place at Dorking Grammar School. It meant having to travel from Epsom to Dorking every day by train and I'd have to buy her a new school uniform – the cost of which, ironically, was fifty pounds. I had to borrow from the bank again to pay for it, but after my own experience of having to wear the ill-fitting second-hand school uniform my mother had bought from a woman in the pub, and of buying a pram and a cot from neighbours when Pat was a baby, I was determined that, this time, she wasn't going to have anyone else's cast-offs.

Peter had started school for the first time, we owed the bank a hundred pounds and, even without the debt, we could barely manage on Roy's income. When I suggested to Roy that I should look for a part-time job, he agreed and, shortly afterwards, I started working in the mornings in the counting-house of a large store in Epsom.

When I arrived at work every day, I had to go round all

the different departments in the store, collecting the big-denomination bank notes from the previous day's takings and then doing the accounting and banking. I loved the job. It was quite well paid, all the other women who worked in the store were friendly, and I thoroughly enjoyed seeing all the new clothes that came in.

I'd learned to drive by that time and sometimes I had to drive to other stores in the area to do spot audits. I left the department store after a while for a new job I'd seen advertised in the local paper as assistant auditor for the South Eastern Electricity Board (SEEB), which subsequently became SEEBOARD. Again, the job involved travelling, this time all round the south-east of England to visit district offices and shops, and not only was the pay better than I'd been earning, it was full-time work, so we were finally able to start making inroads into what we owed the bank. It was unfortunate that while I was travelling around visiting different towns, meeting nice people and doing a job I enjoyed, Roy was stuck in the off-licence, becoming increasingly bored and resentful. But we needed the money I was earning.

I was getting used to the pattern that had developed at home. I was grateful for the 'normal' days, when Roy and I talked to each other and had conversations; but I was always waiting with bated breath for the clouds to start gathering or for the storm of his temper to erupt suddenly without any warning – which it always did eventually.

One autumn day, I'd been doing an audit in Guildford and was driving back to Epsom with a young colleague when I noticed a wooded area of horse chestnut trees. Stopping the car at the side of the road, I said to the young man who was with me, 'I want to get some conkers to take home for my son. It won't take me a minute. I hope you don't mind.'

Peter was seven at the time, and he was delighted when I arrived home with a bag full of big, shiny horse chestnuts, some still encased in their spiky shells. I left him in the dining room, sorting them into piles and polishing them, while I went downstairs to the shop to take over from Roy so that he could have a break.

It was only a few minutes later when I heard Peter screaming. It sounded as though he was in pain and I ran up the stairs from the shop with my heart thudding against my ribs. It took me a few seconds to make sense of what was happening: Peter was cowering in a corner of the room, sobbing, with his arms wrapped tightly round his head, and Roy was thrashing him, raining down blows on his little body with what appeared to be wild, out-of-control fury.

'Stop it!' I had to shout to be heard above the noise they were making. 'Roy! You're hurting him. What's happened? Whatever did he do?'

Roy hit him a couple more times, with less force, and then he stopped.

It turned out that, after emptying his bag of conkers on to the dining table, sorting and polishing them, Peter had begun to hammer holes in them prior to threading them with string. When Roy had come into the room to see what he was doing and had noticed some little scratches on the dining table, he'd exploded into an instant rage.

'He's only seven,' I told Roy. 'He didn't realize what he was doing. It wasn't as though he did it on purpose.' I didn't add, although I could have done, that even if he had, it wouldn't have justified the violence of Roy's attack.

If you live with someone who has a short fuse, you don't ever go blithely through life. It's nerve-racking and emotionally exhausting always having to be careful what you say and always watching for signs that you've inadvertently said the wrong thing. My stomach was constantly tying itself into knots as I scanned every situation for its potential to irritate Roy, so that I could hustle the children out of the way before he turned on them.

There were things going on in the outside world too, of course. It was the early 1960s and it seemed that you couldn't open a newspaper or turn on the radio without reading or hearing about what became known as the Cuban Missile Crisis. John F. Kennedy was President of the USA, and the US Government was focused on fighting what it saw as the major and very real threat of communism. In August 1962, following a couple of failed operations aimed at overthrowing the communist regime in Cuba, a US Air Force plane took photographs of nuclear bases that were being built secretly in Cuba with Soviet aid.

The thirteen-day confrontation that took place in October of that year between the USA on one side and the Soviet Union and Cuba on the other was one of the worst crises of the Cold War. It looked as though the USA and USSR were on a path towards mutual destruction and the world was holding its breath.

The doomsayers were having a field day and Roy became almost panic-stricken. He talked endlessly about how we were all going to be blown up and how the end of the world was nigh. What he said had a terrible effect on Peter, so much so that he became terrified of going to bed at night in case the bombs started falling and we all died horrible deaths in our sleep.

I was in the off-licence one day, trying not to listen to the discussion Roy was having with a customer about the Cuban Crisis, when another customer – a man called Austin who lived in a flat almost directly opposite the shop – came in. Austin listened for a few minutes to the other men's agitated, anxious conversation and then he said, in a quiet, calm voice, 'Well, I work with Americans and I have absolutely no doubt that they're going to come out on top. Believe me: the Russians are going to back down; they know that the Americans are *not* going to give in.'

He seemed to be so certain of what he was saying that even Roy seemed impressed.

'Well, I hope you're right,' he said, sounding almost disappointed; then the conversation came to an end and I breathed a sigh of relief. Perhaps Roy would finally stop worrying about what was going happen to us all and, more importantly, stop talking about it in front of Peter and frightening the poor child so that he couldn't sleep.

Fortunately – for all of us – Austin was right and the

disaster was averted following declarations and agreements, both private and public, on both sides.

I don't think Pat was much affected by Roy's dire warnings of a nuclear holocaust; she didn't seem to take much notice. She was older than Peter, of course, and I think that, by that time, she already had reservations about most of the things Roy said. She kept out of his way as much as she could, although, despite her best efforts, that wasn't always possible and Roy still seemed to find reasons to be annoyed with her.

For example, she was coming home from school on the train one day when she put her head out of the window and her hat blew off. She was a little girl and it was just a mistake. In fact, it was a very fortunate reminder never to put her head out of the window on the train: the consequences could have been much worse.

When I got home from work, the house was in pandemonium. Roy, who was beside himself with fury, was ranting and raving at Pat about how much the hat had cost and how she never took care of the things that were bought for her because she didn't *care* about them or about anything else. It was dreadful, the way he was going on and on at her.

What was even worse, though, was the way she was just standing there, staring down at the ground and flinching as if she was expecting him to hit her every time he jabbed his finger in her face to add more force to his pointless tirade.

'It was an accident,' I told Roy, as soon as I was able to make out what he was shouting about. 'She didn't do it on purpose, did you, Pat? Of course she didn't.' Clearly, Roy didn't care, and, in any case, he wasn't listening.

I ended up in tears and, as soon as she could, Pat escaped to her bedroom, where she spent a good deal of her time when she was at home. For the next few days, Roy laughed, joked and chatted with Peter as normal, and didn't address a single word to either Pat or me.

Nine out of ten times, it wasn't possible to predict what was going to make Roy angry, and on many occasions I never did discover what had caused it. If it was something to do with Pat or me, however tenuously, he wouldn't speak to us for days or even weeks. I'd serve the dinner, we'd all sit at the dining table, and he'd completely ignore us and talk to Peter. Sometimes what he said to Peter was actually something he wanted me to know, but he would refuse to speak to me directly.

It's very difficult to eat when your stomach's churning and your throat seems to be blocked by a solid ball of stress. What I hated most of all, though, was seeing the hurt, incomprehension and then resignation on Pat's face. I don't really know what effect those horrible, angry silences had on Peter; I think most of it went way above his head, because his father was talking to him and because he was too young to be aware of what was happening. I *do* know how they affected Pat: I could almost see the confidence draining out of her and the self-doubt and insecurity rushing in to fill the void.

I felt guilty because of the way he was treating Pat. It was a terrible way to treat any child, and Pat had never, ever, done anything that could possibly have warranted it.

I'd had low self-esteem when I'd married Roy; a few years later, I felt trapped and very unhappy.

I had always got on well with Roy's parents. His mother was one of the sweetest women I'd ever met and I loved her. So I was taken by surprise when I went with Roy and the children to visit them one day and his father suddenly attacked me verbally, for absolutely no reason that I could understand.

Roy had popped out to see his sister, who lived round the corner from their house, when his father began to tell me all the things I did that were wrong. You'd have thought from what he said that I was the worst woman, the worst mother and the worst wife in the entire world. He'd never spoken to me like that before and I was completely shocked.

I still did a lot of knitting at that time, mostly sweaters for the children and Roy. According to my father-in-law, however, buying knitting wool was merely a means of wasting money that should have been spent on other, more useful things. He didn't say what the more useful things were; he'd already moved on to another in a whole list of errors and misdemeanours that, fortunately, I've long since forgotten.

My mother-in-law appeared to be as amazed by her husband's outburst as I was, and she sat there silently, as if mesmerized by what he was saying. It was awful; I felt deeply hurt, stupid and embarrassed. I'd always thought Roy's parents liked me, whereas in reality, it seemed, his father had been storing up for years a whole catalogue of objections and criticisms that he was now giving vent to with angry, undisguised distaste.

Eventually, when he paused for breath, I said, 'Well, I would just like you to know that your son hasn't spoken to me or my daughter for more than two weeks.' I think I said other things too, before standing up, picking up my coat and handbag and running out of the house and down the road to the railway station.

A few minutes later, I was sitting in a seat by the window on a train that would take me home when I saw my father-in-law open the door of a carriage further down the platform. Fortunately, he hadn't seen me and when the train stopped at Epsom, I darted out of the station and walked quickly down the road towards the bus stop.

Whatever my father-in-law was intending to do, I knew he wouldn't be able to follow me up the stairs of the bus. I found a seat near the back and sat there, wiping the tears from my cheeks with the sleeve of my coat as I tried to make sense of the jumble of half-thoughts in my head and willed the bus driver to start the engine. I was still sitting there when I heard heavy footsteps on the stairs and then Roy's cold, angry voice say, 'Get – Down – Stairs.'

He didn't speak a single word to me as I sat beside him in his van. So I didn't know until we got home that he'd already picked up his father and taken him there.

'I've come to apologize,' my father-in-law told me. 'I'm very sorry for the things I said.' He didn't offer any explanation; he just kept saying he was sorry and then, 'I'd better go now. Don't worry, son, I'll catch the bus.'

'I'll walk down the road with you to the bus stop,' I said,

hoping that if we walked there together, one of us might be able to think of something to say that would make everything all right again.

My mother-in-law had recently been in hospital having an operation, and as soon as we were out of the house my father-in-law said, 'Lil being unwell hasn't been easy for me, you know.'

'I understand that,' I told him. 'And I'm sorry. What I *don't* understand is why you'd take that out on me. I'm not to blame for Lil's illness.'

We walked the rest of the way in silence and when I got home Roy didn't speak to me either. It was several days before things settled down again, as they always did eventually. Pat told me later that she and Peter had been very frightened sitting in the back of Roy's van that day while he sped through the streets on the way home from his parents' house. I never did find out what, specifically, had made him angry: I don't think Lil ever told him what his father had said to me.

Becoming aware that you've fallen out of love with someone is very, very sad. Although the realization itself might be abrupt, the process that leads up to it isn't something that happens overnight. I suppose, for me, the seeds were sown on the day Roy stood on Pat's fingers and told her he didn't like her. For the next few years, he was rarely nice to Pat and as his demoralizing silences became longer and more frequent, the stress increased steadily for both of us.

We lived permanently on tenterhooks, always wondering

if we were going to get through the day without any major upsets. In the end, I looked forward to going to work – as I expect Pat looked forward to going to school; I was grateful to have a reason to be out of the house all day and to be doing something I enjoyed.

I suppose everyone's breaking point is different. After the first time Roy was so awful to Pat, I couldn't bring myself to accept that he wasn't the man I'd believed him to be and that I'd made a mistake. I loved Roy at that time, so I told myself that what had happened was *my* fault in some way. As the years passed and he became nastier, so that placating him became more difficult, I had to search deeper and deeper inside myself for the love I used to feel for him, until I looked and it simply wasn't there any more.

It was after Roy had been particularly horrible one day that I told him I was leaving him. Pat and I spent that night at a friend's house. I didn't take Peter with me because I knew Roy wouldn't let me leave with him and that if I tried to do so Peter would just be even more upset. So I left him that night, although I had no intention of leaving permanently without him.

The friend Pat and I stayed with was also a friend of Roy's and I knew she felt awkward about getting in the middle of what was going on between us. I'd have to find somewhere for myself and the children to live as soon as possible.

When I arrived for work at the SEEB on the Monday morning, Roy was waiting for me in the car park.

'I don't want to talk to you,' I told him. 'There's nothing for either of us to say.'

'Please,' he begged me. 'Come home. Don't leave me.

Please, Sheila. It'll be different, I promise. I love you. I don't want to be without you. Peter keeps asking where you are, and he misses Pat. Please, Sheila. Please come home.'

Sometimes you believe what you want to believe. Or perhaps what really happens is that when you want something to be true, you allow yourself to hope that it might be. So Pat and I went home, and for a few weeks things *were* better.

Roy's family used to come and stay with us at Christmas, and while they were there that year, Roy came upstairs to the flat and started shouting about something in the way he often did. Later, when he'd gone back down to the off-licence, his sister, Ruby, came into the kitchen where I was making a pot of tea and asked me, 'Sheila, why don't you *ever* say anything? Why do you let him do that to you?'

'Because I hate confrontation,' I answered. 'And it wouldn't get me anywhere if I *did* say something. That's just how he is, Ruby. He isn't going to change.'

'Well, I don't know about that,' Ruby said. 'But I *do* think you should stand up to him.'

She was probably right and that *is* what I should have done – for Pat's and Peter's sakes even more than for my own. I didn't though. Not because I was afraid of Roy – at least, not physically afraid in that I thought he would ever hit me. It was because conflict, quarrels and angry shouting always made me feel sick and faint; the palms of my hands would sweat and my head would feel as though it was filling up with some sort of dense gas that stopped me being able to think clearly.

After Christmas, when Roy's family left and we were on

our own again, the atmosphere returned to what I'd learned to accept as normal.

The day after they'd gone, I opened the rubbish bin to put something inside it and there on top of the damp, evil-smelling waste were all the presents Pat had given Roy for Christmas. For a moment, I just stood and looked at them, trying to think of some explanation, however implausible. When I went back into the house and asked Pat if she knew why the presents were in the bin, she looked at me with tears in her eyes and said, 'No, I don't know why they're there. I found them on my bed this morning, and I put them on the tallboy in your bedroom.'

When Roy came up from the shop, I asked him the same question and he answered, 'I don't want them. I want nothing from her ever again.'

This time, as well as the sick, heavy feeling in the pit of my stomach, I felt something else: I knew I'd finally made a decision I should have made a long time ago.

'May God forgive you for what you've done,' I told Roy, 'because I never will. I'm leaving you.'

16

It was when I told Roy I was leaving that he told me about the two hundred pounds his father had lent him. Apparently, he'd been drinking again and he'd needed the money urgently to repay the cost of what he'd taken from the off-licence because he'd heard that the company was going to do a stock-take. If they'd found out what he'd been doing, they'd have sacked him.

'I had to go to my parents and ask them to bale me out,' he told me. 'My father was furious. But he gave me the money I needed to set the books right. I didn't want you to know about it, so I made them promise not to tell you.'

Maybe that was the explanation, at least in part, for his father's angry outburst against me that day. Perhaps Roy had made excuses for his stealing that had led his father to believe I was somehow responsible for whatever his problem was. I'd done a lot of things wrong in my life, but I didn't think I could reasonably be held to blame for that: if Roy was unhappy, he wasn't the only one.

'I'm sorry,' I told Roy, and it was true, for lots of reasons. 'I'm really shocked to know that you did it again. It doesn't really change anything though. I've already decided that I want a divorce.'

'The problem is . . .' There was an expression of almost child-like guilt on his face. 'The problem is that I've done it again. I don't know what's wrong with me, Sheila. I owe the firm another two hundred. My father won't lend me any more money and I don't know what to do.'

Roy was earning about twelve pounds a week and I was bringing home another ten, which meant that our total income was less than ninety pounds a month. Even allowing for the fact that our accommodation was free, two hundred pounds was a ridiculously large sum of money to have spent on *anything*.

After what had happened at Chessington, I suppose it was stupid of me not to have kept a check on things. But I really thought he'd learned his lesson and I don't think it even crossed my mind he'd do it again. Suddenly, I was too weary to be angry.

'I just can't go on doing this,' I said at last. 'I'm unhappy, the children are unhappy, and I can only assume that you are, too; otherwise why *would* you have done it again? Why would you have risked your job and put us in debt for such a huge sum of money? I don't understand, Roy. What's *really* sad, though, is that I don't want to try to understand any more: I don't care why you did it. The only thing that matters now is what you do next – and even that doesn't matter to *me*. In fact, there's only one thing you *can* do: you'll have to go to Head Office and tell them about it yourself.'

It was as if a band of cold, hard steel had closed round my heart. I think Roy must have sensed the way I felt, because instead of shouting at me as he'd normally have done if I'd dared to confront him, he said again that he was sorry and that he'd do what I'd suggested. As he stood there in front of me like a miserable, contrite little boy, I did feel sorry for him. I felt angry and guilty, too: I should have ended our marriage years ago instead of allowing Pat to be exposed for ten years to Roy's outbursts of unreasonable temper and to his repeated, protracted, confidence-crushing silences when he refused to speak to her or to me.

I knew that as soon as he went to Head Office and told them what he'd done, the company would send someone to change the locks on the shop and do a stock-take. What I also knew was that they couldn't lock the children and me out of our home and turn us out on to the street immediately, which meant I had a few days, at least, to find somewhere else to live.

When I went to work the next day, I took a deep breath and told my boss what had happened.

'I'm leaving my husband,' I said. 'I don't know where the children and I will go when we're put out of the flat, which is what will happen sooner or later.'

'You must go to the council straight away,' my boss retorted. 'They'll find somewhere for you and the children to live. It'll be all right, Sheila. Don't you worry about it. It will all work out in the end.'

I wished I could believe him.

I did take his advice and go the council offices in my lunch break that same day, where I was told not to move out of the flat until the council had found other accommodation for me and the children.

Roy moved into digs near the off-licence and within a very short time I'd been allocated a prefab house just round the corner. It couldn't have been in a better position: the children could continue going to the same schools, which meant that they didn't have to start all over again and make new friends; I had the same journey to work; and Peter would be near his father, which I knew was what both of them would want.

When I'd told Roy I was going to divorce him, he'd made me promise to wait.

'Just think about it for six months,' he begged me. 'Don't do anything yet. Give me a chance to make you change your mind. Don't make a decision now, when you're angry with me.'

I wasn't really angry with him – just bemused and exhausted – but I did agree to wait.

I really thought I'd be able to manage on my own: I was earning a reasonable salary – enough to be able to look after myself and the two children – and we had somewhere to live. I'd already begun to work through the terrible sense of anguish and loss you feel when you realize your marriage is over, and I knew I didn't need Roy in my life. More importantly, nor did Pat. For Peter, however, it was going to be an entirely different matter.

Pat was fifteen and Peter was seven when the three of us moved into the prefab. Pat didn't talk about what had happened; in fact, she didn't talk about Roy at all – at least, not to me. Fortunately, she had Chris. Chris and Pat had been friends since the day they met at the grammar school; then he'd become her boyfriend and someone she could confide in and rely on. Many years later, Chris told me that it had taken a very long time for Pat to shake off the effects of Roy's treatment of her. I sometimes used to wonder if she'd ever get over it and regain her sense of self-worth.

I felt very guilty about what Pat had had to deal with, and I still do. On the day that she was born, when I'd looked into her face for the first time and decided I was going to keep her, I'd been determined that, somehow, I was going to give her a good life – as good, if not better, than the life she might have had if she'd been adopted. What I'd actually given her – indirectly – was a life that resulted in her having the same low level of self-esteem I'd always had. At least she had a mother who loved her. I just hoped that, through all the miserable times, she'd always known that.

A few days after we'd moved into the prefab, I told Pat, 'I'm going to get cross with you sometimes and I'm going to tell you off. But I promise you that there'll be no sulking and no bad temper. I'll say what I want to say to you and then it'll be over and done with.'

I recognized the sound of my own weariness in Pat's sigh when she said, 'Oh Mum, those *dreadful* silences.'

'I know, darling,' I answered. 'I promise we're not going to have them any more.'

Getting away from Roy was a very positive thing for Pat, whereas Peter's reaction to being separated from his father was heart-breaking. Peter was extremely upset by what had happened, which was understandable in view of the relationship he had with Roy, who treated him very differently from the way he treated Pat and me. After we left, Peter often cried and asked me, 'Why can't we all live together again with Dad?' Even if it was a question that was prompted by Roy, it was still a true reflection of the way Peter felt, and I hated having to tell him, 'I'm sorry, darling; we just can't.'

After a while, Roy got a job in Surrey and moved into a flat with some other people, and Peter stayed with him there every weekend. I didn't wait six months before seeing a solicitor. Although I'd promised Roy I would, it was a promise I hadn't really had any intention of keeping because I knew with complete certainty that I wasn't going to change my mind. I'd started divorce proceedings almost as soon as I'd moved with the children into the prefab. Roy was very upset with me when the papers were served on him.

'You promised you'd wait,' he said bitterly.

All I could say was, 'I know I did. I'm sorry. But I knew what I wanted to do, so there didn't seem to be any point.'

A few weeks before Pat's sixteenth birthday, I received a tax rebate of forty pounds. There were lots of things I could have spent the money on; however, I knew exactly what I was going to do with it.

'You're only sweet sixteen once,' I told Pat. 'And we're going to celebrate.'

We moved most of the furniture out of the house and put it in a tent in the garden, and then we threw a party. For me, it was like putting a full stop at the end of writing on a piece of paper, then turning it over and holding the pen above a new, empty page on which I could write whatever I wanted to write. As well as being a landmark birthday, it was an important occasion for Pat for another reason too, as it was during her party that she and Chris announced they were 'going steady' and were going to get married as soon as they left school.

Of course, it wasn't simply a case of leaving Roy and starting a new, better life without him. I'm sure getting divorced is never that easy. Ending a marriage might be the solution to one problem, but I imagine, for most people, it's also just the beginning of many others, both practical and emotional. After I left Roy, I felt guilty about Pat, worried about separating Peter from his father, anxious about how I was going to manage financially, and as if I'd failed. Despite all the guilt and anxiety, I thought I was dealing with everything quite well, under the circumstances. It was a conversation I had on the phone with my brother Eddie that made me realize that, in reality, my emotions were still in a state of hopeless turmoil.

'I'm going to divorce Roy,' I told him.

'Why would you do that?' Eddie asked brusquely. 'After all, he was good enough to marry you.'

It was like a slap in the face, particularly coming from the one brother with whom I'd always remained very close. Was that what everyone thought: that a fallen woman like me had been lucky to find any man willing to overlook her sins and make, if not a decent woman, then at least a married woman of her? When you'd made a 'mistake' like the one I'd made, how long did you have to wait before people treated you fairly? Or did that never happen?

*

When we moved into the prefab, Peter was delighted to find that a little boy called David, who he'd become friendly with when we were living above the off-licence, lived next door. I was pleased too, because it meant that there was at least one thing about the move that wasn't horrible for him.

I was going to work every day, and the woman who worked at the dry-cleaner's in the parade of shops very kindly offered to look after Peter until I got home. She wouldn't take any money for looking after him; she said it was company for her two little girls, one of whom, particularly, was the apple of her eye.

One afternoon, when I went to pick Peter up as usual, the woman said to me, 'You need to give him a good hiding when you get him home.' I was shocked, both by the suggestion itself and by the vehemence of her tone. It turned out that Peter had done something to upset the little girl she favoured. I can't remember now what it was, although I do remember that it seemed to be something fairly minor and unintentional.

'I'm sorry,' I told her, 'but I can't do that. If you felt that he needed to be punished, you should have dealt with it at the time. I can't smack him now – in cold blood – for something he did when I wasn't there.'

She wasn't very pleased with me, and although she said she was happy to continue to have Peter after school, our relationship became a bit strained after that and I felt awkward when I went to pick him up.

Peter used to walk to school with his friend David from next door. One day, when I went into the local post office, one of the assistants said to me, 'I don't want to worry you, Mrs Muller, but Peter seems to be spending a lot of money in the shop.'

'I don't understand,' I told her. 'He doesn't have any money. I don't know what you mean.'

It's funny how sometimes it isn't the really big things that tip the balance: all the small, apparently trivial things can add up, almost without you noticing them, until the last little one sends everything crashing out of kilter. As I stood there in the post office, it suddenly felt as though all the worries that had been been building up were pressing down on me like weights.

I could see that the woman was uncertain whether to go on. I think she'd only said something because she felt sympathetic and was trying to be helpful, so after a moment she said, 'He's spending a whole shilling every morning.'

'Well, he isn't getting from me!' The shock that was clearly audible in my voice only increased her discomfort.

Later that day, I sat down at the kitchen table with Peter and told him, 'I need to talk to you about something. I understand you're buying a lot of sweeties these days. Where are you getting the money from?'

'David's giving it to me,' he answered warily, but without any sign of guilt.

'And where is David getting the money from?' I persisted.

'I don't know.' Peter shrugged in the eloquent way children do when they decide an adult is making an unnecessary fuss.

I believed him, so I went and knocked on our neighbours' door and told David's mother what had happened. 'I don't know where the money's coming from,' I said. 'I just don't want Peter to have it.'

'Oh dear,' David's mother said, 'I'm afraid I can guess. His father has been collecting coins in a big bottle and I think David might have been taking money from that.'

It wasn't a terrible thing, certainly not on Peter's behalf, because he wouldn't ever have thought to ask where his friend was getting the money and he hadn't known he was taking it without his parents' permission. But despite the explanation and Peter's lack of culpability in what had happened, it threw me into a terrible state. I knew how upset Peter had been by the break-up of our family and I began to imagine all sorts of dreadful things that could happen to him in the future, all the wrong paths he could take, because I'd taken him away from his father and because I was at work when he came home from school and therefore not there to look after him.

I lost my confidence completely and felt that I wasn't able to cope with him. I was making a mess of things and I was failing Peter. It was a huge overreaction, which resulted in my making a huge mistake.

I went to see Roy, told him about David and the money and then said, heatedly, 'You're always saying you want Peter to live with you, although you never do anything to make that possible. When he stays with you at the weekends you spoil him, and then it takes me the rest of the week to sort him out again. Now this has happened. Well, the time has come for you to put your words into action and look after him. Peter needs to live with you now. '

I can't believe I did it. Roy loved Peter, there's no question about that, and he continued to love him more than he'd ever loved anyone until the day he died. But *I* was Peter's mother, and I loved him too, although he'd have been forgiven for thinking I didn't after I'd pushed him away like that. I won't ever forgive myself. All I can say in my defence is that I *wasn't* myself at that time.

I felt swamped by worries. I thought I was doing a poor job of trying to cope with them and that, having allowed Pat to suffer emotionally while I was married to Roy, I was now being a bad parent to my son. I wasn't thinking straight and I felt guilty about almost everything. It was guilt that was only compounded by sending my son to live with his father.

Roy must have told his solicitor that Peter had started to live with him and I got a very sternly worded letter from *my* solicitor saying that what I'd done was wrong and I'd flouted the ruling of the court, which stated that Peter was to live with me. However, despite everyone's disapproval of what I'd done, Peter stayed with Roy.

I loved both my children with all my heart, which made it even more difficult to come to terms with the thought that I'd done just about everything wrong.

17

My brother Eric had barely spoken to me since the day he'd taken me to the solicitor after finding out I was pregnant. I hadn't seen him for a long time when Pat and I bumped into him on the street while we were visiting other members of my family in Rotherham. He spoke to me as if nothing had ever happened and then he turned to Pat – who was sixteen and who he hadn't seen since she was a toddler at my mother's house – and asked, in a jovial, avuncular tone, 'And how's my favourite niece?'

Pat just looked at him without answering. Later, when we'd gone our separate ways, she almost exploded with indignation.

'I wanted to spit in his eye!' she cried. 'How *dare* he say that to me? How dare he call me his favourite niece when he's refused all these years even to acknowledge my existence? Who does he think he's fooling?'

She was furious, and I felt hurt and insulted on her behalf, although I think Eric had only said what he'd said because he was embarrassed. Pat didn't know him from Adam and I suppose he'd been caught off guard and didn't know *what* to say. It was stupid of him, and he wasn't a stupid man. However, he probably was a man who found anything emotional difficult to cope with. Perhaps that's why he'd turned his back on me so coldly and decisively all those years ago. It was the same for all our mother's children: blocking out our emotions and just 'getting on with it' was something we were good at.

One afternoon, while Peter was still living with Pat and me in the prefab, I'd called in at the dry-cleaner's to collect him on my way home from work when I bumped into Austin, the man who'd spoken with such calm authority in the off-licence that day when Roy had been talking about the Cuban Crisis.

Divorce wasn't very common, even in the mid-sixties, and – like politics and religion – it was deemed to be a bit of an embarrassing subject to discuss, so people tended to avoid mentioning it. Austin's kindness overcame the usual constraints, however, and he smiled sympathetically as he said, 'I'm divorced myself, so I know it's a very traumatic thing to go through. If you'd like to go to the cinema one evening, I'd be very happy to take you.'

'That would be nice,' I told him. 'Thank you. I'd like that.'

I was thirty-five and Austin was sixty-three. I didn't know his age at that time – he looked considerably younger – but I knew that he was just being kind. After the cinema, we went out to dinner; then we went out again and became friends. He was a very handsome, very interesting man, and it wasn't long before our friendship developed into something more.

When the council started emptying the prefabs – which had already long outlived their expected lifespan – Pat and I moved into a two-bedroom flat on the top floor of a new block in Tattenham Corner, a small town in Surrey that's home to Epsom Downs Racecourse. It was a very nice flat, so I don't think there was any deep psychological reason why I kept locking myself out of it!

The first time it happened was on the day we were moving in. Austin had come to see our new home and had offered to take Pat to a doctor's appointment, so that I could get on with unpacking boxes. They hadn't been gone long when I stepped outside the front door and heard it click shut behind me.

I tried everything I could think of to open it – although, in fact, I couldn't think of very much. And then one of the men who'd been helping with the move pushed a long bit of wire through the letterbox, managed to wrap the end of it round the catch on the lock inside and pulled the door open. It seemed best not to ask how he'd learned and perfected such a skill!

The next time I locked myself out was when I was off work for a couple of days suffering from sunstroke. I'd taken Pat and Peter to Brighton for the day one Sunday and hadn't realized until I got up to go to work the next morning that my back and neck had been badly burned by the sun while we were sitting on the beach.

I drove to work feeling light-headed and slightly sick, and then one of the engineers drove me home again shortly afterwards when I began to feel very ill. Back in the flat, I crawled into bed and stayed there for the next couple of days, until I felt well enough, just, to go out to do some shopping.

When I got back to the flat, I put the shopping bags down on the landing outside the front door while I opened it, took some of the bags into the kitchen, put the catch down on the door and went back out on to the landing to pick up the rest. At least, that's what I thought I'd done. What I'd actually done was put the keys on the kitchen table and not quite clicked the catch on the front door into place, which had allowed it to close behind me. I couldn't believe I'd locked myself out again. This time, there was no one around to help me.

When I went out on to the street, I saw a man walking away down the road with a ladder balanced on his shoulder. Fortunately, I still had my car keys in my pocket, so I jumped in the car and followed him. When I caught up with him, I drove slowly along beside him, trying to attract his attention, and when he eventually turned to look at me, I think he thought he was being followed by a crazy woman and he quickened his pace. He did finally stop, although I suspect he wished he hadn't when he was accosted by a flushed, agitated woman who, without any preamble or explanation, asked him, like some music-hall comedian, 'How long is your ladder?'

After I'd explained my predicament, pointed towards the block of flats and told him that mine was on the third floor, he looked at me with a puzzled expression and said, 'I'm sorry, love, but it's not long enough to reach right up there.' He was right, of course: I think the effects of the sunstroke hadn't worn off as much as I'd thought they had. I apologized and he walked away, shaking his head and leaving me feeling stupid and helpless, with no idea what to do. Then it struck me: I'd phone the fire brigade.

First, they sent a man out in a van. I stood with him as he shielded the sun from his eyes with his hand and looked up at the block of flats, then scratched his head and asked, 'Are there any windows open?'

'Yes,' I told him eagerly, sensing that he was formulating a solution to the problem. 'The sitting-room window is open. It's down the side of the building.'

'Hmm.' He scratched his head again. 'Well, I haven't got anything that'll reach up there, love. Don't worry, though; we'll get you in.'

He made a phone call and a few minutes later another van arrived, followed by a fire engine. By the time one of the firemen had climbed up a very long ladder and in through the open window, I was beginning to feel sick and my head was throbbing – this time, the effects of sunstroke exacerbated by acute embarrassment. I learned my lesson, however, and I haven't ever locked myself out again!

Pat and I lived in that flat together until she married Chris, the boy who had been first her friend at the age of eleven and then her boyfriend. I didn't support their decision to get married when they did. In fact, I was quite a misery about it. They were both twenty, which I thought was much too young: I was sure it would all end in tears.

I desperately wanted to protect Pat and stop her making mistakes that would cause her to be hurt in the way I'd been hurt by my own mistakes. Pat wasn't me, though; and Chris wasn't Roy. Forty-two years and two beautiful children later, they're still very happy together – which just goes to show what *I* know about anything. I'm so grateful that Chris came into her life when he did. Rebuilding the self-confidence she'd started to lose when she was just five years old and Roy stepped on her fingers was a long, slow process, and it was Chris who helped her to do it.

While Pat and Chris were happy together in a mutually supportive and loving relationship, things were going well between me and Austin too.

I'd loved George, the boy I'd met and danced with when I was at school and who I'd been engaged to. I hadn't loved Pat's father: I'd just been flattered by his attention after George had broken off our engagement and I'd believed it was my fault and I was unlovable. I'd been in love with Roy when I married him, and I'd stayed in love with him for some time – or, at least, I'd stayed in love with the man I thought he was. But it was only with Austin that I finally knew what it meant to have a truly loving relationship – to love a man and to be loved by him.

I had a job as an assistant accountant that I really enjoyed and Austin travelled a lot for the work he did for the American Port of Maryland. He was a very intelligent man and an excellent raconteur with plenty of stories to tell. Even young people, such as Pat, Chris and their friends, enjoyed talking and listening to him, and the fact that he got on so well with Peter, Pat and Chris – and, later, with Pat and Chris's children too – was wonderful for me.

For seven years, Austin and I were together, leading our own lives while at the same time becoming entangled in each other's, and we were very happy. He never talked about getting married. What he *would* sometimes say was, 'I'm far too old for you. Why don't you find someone else, someone closer to your own age?'

'I don't *want* anyone else,' I'd always protest. 'The difference in our ages doesn't matter to me. Really, it doesn't.'

Although it didn't feel as though he was trying to push me away, it hurt me when he said it. Perhaps I could hear just the faintest whisper of a voice in my head reminding me what had happened when Ernie Burns finally became 'free' to marry my mother after she'd waited all those years for him. What Austin and I had together wasn't anything like their furtive liaison: I was content and secure in my relationship with him. However, after seven years, I thought, 'He's right. I really do need to do something about this. I'm never going to persuade him that the age difference doesn't matter, and he isn't going to change his mind. I'm forty-two and if I want to get married again, I'm going to have to take his advice and go and find someone else.'

We were having dinner in my flat one evening when I told him, 'I've been thinking about what you're always saying and I think you're right. I've decided I'm going to finish this.' I didn't want to cry and make him feel bad, but there were tears in my eyes when I touched his arm lightly with my fingers and said, 'I *am* going to try to find someone else. It isn't because . . .'

'No!' Austin grabbed my hand and held it so tightly he almost crushed it. 'No, you can't do that! Please, Sheila, don't do that. We'll get married. Don't find someone else. Please!'

216

It turned out that that was what he'd wanted all along, but he'd felt guilty about the idea of tying me to a much older man.

We were married on 28 September 1973. It was a day that still sits right alongside the other two best days of my life – the days when my children were born.

18

I didn't have much contact with my mother as she got older. I hadn't seen her for years when my sister Mabel phoned me one day and said, 'She's had a mini-stroke. She's in hospital. You ought to come.'

When I arrived at the hospital the next day, my mother was sitting up in bed, laughing and making jokes while she squeezed a ball in each hand to improve the grip of her fingers. I shouldn't have felt irritated, but I'd had to take time off work and drive all the way from Epsom to Rotherham, and somehow, the sight of her sitting there, as bright as anything, brought to the surface – just for a moment – the resentment towards her that was usually buried deep inside me.

I think the last time I'd seen her before that day was when I took Peter for a visit and we'd stayed with her in the flat she was still living in when she had the stroke. On that occasion, it had quickly become clear that she wasn't eating properly, so I'd bought food and cooked us all a good meal. When we sat down to eat it, I was appalled by her manners, particularly in front of Peter. It was almost as if she was doing it deliberately. Suddenly, I felt completely alienated from her. We were living in different worlds. Ever since I could remember, I'd wanted to escape from the world she'd created around us when we were children, and all I could think as I watched her eat the food I'd cooked was, 'I don't want to be here. I want to get away.'

The hardest thing of all for me to face was the fact that I had no feeling of love for her at all; I'm sure that she had none for me. We'd stumbled along through the years trying not to do too much harm to each other, but we were poles apart in every way – in our nature, our thinking, everything.

I love my children more than anything or anyone in the world. I'd gladly, without a second thought, lay down my life to protect them. To this day, I still feel guilty and deeply regretful about every sadness and heartache they've experienced in their lives. Loving them wasn't something I had to learn or teach myself to do; it was something that came naturally, instinctively. I've felt it for each of them from the moment I set eyes on them. So *how* did my mother not feel that way about me? The answer to that question has remained a mystery to me throughout my entire life.

I didn't see her again for some time after that visit to the hospital, not until after Austin and I were married and went up to Rotherham to see my brother Eddie and his wife Iris, by which time my mother was living in an old people's home.

When we arrived there, she was sitting in a chair in the room she shared with another old lady. I was shocked by the change in her physical appearance. She'd become very fat and, as she was quite a short woman, her body seemed to have lost any recognizable shape and was almost square.

There was a dreadful smell in the room, the same smell that seemed to permeate every corner of every room in the building. It made me feel quite nauseous and I suggested we should all go and sit outside, in the fresh air.

We'd been sitting in the garden for a few minutes when a couple walked across the grass towards the building and my mother made a horrible, crude remark about them. I thought for a moment that I was actually going to be sick. Eddie and Iris's teenage son had come with us and I glanced at him quickly, praying he hadn't heard the disgusting thing his grandmother had said. Fortunately, Austin was speaking to him quietly, pointing at something in the distance, and both of them seemed blissfully ignorant of what had just occurred.

I looked at my mother. The expression on her face was one of complacent self-satisfaction. 'She hasn't changed at all,' I thought. 'In fact, she's getting worse as she gets older.' And why wouldn't she have been? I don't know why I thought she might have been any different.

As I sat there in the sunshine, I realized I'd lived my whole life trying to do what I'd been brought up to do – ignore and repress my true feelings and just get on with things; now it was time to accept the facts. The truth was that she hadn't been a good mother, to any of us, and she wasn't a nice person. She wasn't ever going to change and she wasn't ever going to do me anything except harm – emotionally, at least. It's a horrible thing to say about one's own mother; but then, as I've said before, things *are* what they *are* and there's no point wishing – or pretending – they're any different.

That was the last time I saw her alive. She died not long afterwards, in 1978, at the age of eighty-four. I went to the funeral, because she was my mother. Sadly, though, I don't think many tears were shed at her passing.

Austin met several members of my family – Eddie, particularly, liked him very much – but that was the only time he ever met my mother. He was as polite and pleasant to her as he was to everyone, and although I did sometimes talk to him about her, I never asked him what he thought of her, and he didn't ever volunteer an opinion.

Austin had retired shortly after we got married, when he was seventy. After retirement, he was just as busy as he'd ever been, doing voluntary work at the local hospital three days a week and playing golf every weekend. There's so much I could write about the things we did and the time we had together – the holidays, the laughter and the pure pleasure of sitting on the sofa in the evening beside the man you love and who loves you. It wouldn't be interesting though; not to anyone else.

Sometimes, people are content without really being aware of it: they just accept it as the norm. In my case, however, I was very aware of how happy Austin and I were together. I had a lot of unhappiness to compare it to. Austin really appreciated being married and looked after. Not long after our wedding, he told me, 'We should have done this a long time ago. What a pity we didn't know one another when we were younger. It would have been lovely to have had children with you.' And I felt the same way: it was as if I was finally where I was supposed to be, with the person I should always have been with.

Austin empowered me. It was the first time in my life someone had done that. He'd say things to me no one had ever said to me before, and almost every morning he'd look at me as though he was really seeing me and say, 'You look beautiful this morning, darling.' When he looked at me like that, it was as if I had been suddenly suffused in a bright light. He was kind, thoughtful and generous in every way, and I felt cherished and, finally, *loved*.

I didn't care if anyone thought Austin was too old for me. Being married to him allowed me to be myself: I could say what I wanted to say and do what I wanted to do without being afraid of upsetting him or making him angry. We talked to each other – about the good things and the bad things – and the atmosphere was never heavy with silent, inexplicable disapproval.

Pat was completely at ease with Austin, too. He treated her like a daughter and was truly fond of her. I was so grateful to him for being the father-figure I'd always wanted for her. She had Chris's father, of course; he'd always been good to her since she and Chris first became friends. But I was very happy to know that she now had Austin as well. Peter liked him too, although it wasn't the same for him, because he had a relationship with a father who loved him, and he didn't *need* to have someone like Austin in his life, as I felt Pat did.

Austin and I had our moments, of course. They never involved sulking or being deliberately hurtful; they were just the sort of hiccups any two people are likely to have when they're learning to live together. For example, there was the occasion when I decided to paint the kitchen . . .

We hadn't been married for very long and Austin was out playing golf when the idea came to me. I drove into Epsom to buy some paint and when Austin came home I was hard at work. I called out to him when I heard the front door opening, and as he walked into the kitchen, the smile on his face wavered and then his expression became wary.

'What are you doing?' he asked me, although I'd have thought the answer was self-evident.

'I thought the kitchen could do with a new coat of paint,' I said cheerfully, waving the paintbrush in the general direction of the cupboard doors I'd just completed.

'You didn't ask *me*,' he responded.

'I didn't realize I *had* to ask you!' I laughed.

'What sort of paint is it?' he asked, ignoring what I'd said.

'It's a new type of paint,' I told him, my confidence starting to falter. 'It's called Vymura. It's really good.'

Austin made a dismissive, air-expelling noise, looked from the pot of paint to the door of the cupboard that, until a few seconds ago, I'd been so proud of, and said, 'That won't last five minutes. You can't use any old paint in a kitchen. You should have asked me about it first. It isn't . . .'

Still holding the paintbrush in my hand, I ran into the bathroom, locked the door and sat on the toilet, crying my eyes out.

When I'd recovered my composure, I blew my nose,

washed the paint off my hands and went into the kitchen to make sandwiches for our lunch. While we were eating them, Austin said sheepishly, 'I'll give you a hand in the kitchen afterwards, darling, if you'd like me to.'

Later, as I was putting the finishing touches to the paintwork, he picked up the pot of Vymura and said, 'This is actually really nice paint.' For weeks afterwards, when anyone came to the flat, he'd say to them, 'We used that new Vymura paint in the kitchen. It really is wonderful.' It still makes me laugh when I think about it today. He was right though: that paint remained on those doors in pristine condition for years!

I'd become so used to living on my own and doing whatever I wanted to do that it hadn't occurred to me to ask Austin's permission to do some *painting*. But he'd lived on his own for a long time too, and that incident reminded both of us that we weren't two single people sharing a house: we were living *together*.

There were other points that Austin was not so willing to concede. Before and during our marriage, we'd both amassed quite a lot of ornaments and mementoes that we'd arranged around the house on windowsills, tables and mantelpieces. If I ever moved any of them, they'd very quickly be returned to their original position. The first couple of times it happened, I was mildly irritated by it – until I realized that not being able to move ornaments around the house on a whim was a very small price to pay for even a tiny part of the happiness Austin brought into my life.

*

We'd been married for seven years, and together for nineteen, when Austin was diagnosed with lymphoma. He told me some time later that after he'd been given the diagnosis, he'd looked it up in a book at the hospital where he did voluntary work and read that the average survival time for the condition he had was five years.

He was treated with steroids and eventually had so many blood transfusions that his blood vessels became weak and began to burst, causing internal haemorrhaging. He died on 8 October 1985, at the age of eighty-two, almost exactly five years after his diagnosis.

I was devastated. We seemed to have had such a short time together. I'd known all along that I wouldn't grow old with Austin beside me – it was the reason he'd been reluctant to 'tie' me to him before we were married. But *knowing* something's going to happen doesn't make it any easier when it does. I tried to remind myself that it was better to have had nineteen years of happiness with him than none at all. And although I know that's true, it didn't make losing him any less painful or less hard to bear.

Pat and Chris's children, my grandson and granddaughter, Toby and Sammie, loved Austin too. Toby, who was just a little boy when Austin died, was inconsolable at his funeral. When he said something about losing his grandfather, Pat told him gently, 'He wasn't really your granddad, Toby,' which made the poor child cry even more.

'Of course he's our granddad!' Toby sobbed.

'No, he isn't really,' Pat persisted.

'What do you mean "He isn't really"? He's always been our granddad,' Toby said.

I think Pat was saying it because she didn't want to upset Austin's daughter, who was also at the funeral. Toby was right though: Austin had been part of our family since before Chris and Pat's children were born and, to them, he *was* Granddad.

After Austin died, I stayed in the maisonette in Epsom where we'd lived together, and continued to work at the firm of insurance brokers I'd been with for some time. It was interesting work and I'd always enjoyed doing it. Now, though, it was just part of what had become an existence without any real point. I'd come home to an empty flat, get something to eat, wait until it was late enough to be a reasonable time to go to bed, get up the next morning, go to work, come home . . . They say time is a great healer; I really hoped that was true.

I tried to keep myself busy: I did a tapestry and I even took part in a fashion show at a local shop. After the show, the woman who ran the shop asked if I'd be interested in working there on Saturdays. I laughed and told her I already had a job, but she was persistent.

'You're always so well turned out,' she said. 'You've got a good eye for colour, and you obviously like clothes.' And in the end I agreed: at least it would be a way of distracting myself for a few hours from focusing on my grief and on the emptiness Austin had left behind him when he went.

My Saturday job didn't last very long, however. When I arrived on the first day and the woman told me to vacuum the room upstairs where the staff made cups of tea, I knew my days there were numbered. If I'd wanted to clean, I could have done it at home – and vacuuming wasn't really something that required a 'good eye for colour'. I stuck it out for a few weeks and then made my excuses and left.

It was less than a year after Austin's death when I was made redundant from the job I loved at the company where I'd been working for twelve years. It was a complete shock to me when I was called in to the chief accountant's office one Friday afternoon and told that I was being 'let go'. In fact, the company was beginning to crumble for various reasons, and it didn't survive much longer after I left – which isn't to suggest that the two events were connected in any way!

I got another auditing job almost immediately, and then that too came to an end a few months later, when the company relocated to Dorking and I decided not to make the move with it.

One day when I was feeling sorry for myself, I thought, 'All I'm doing is going to work, coming home; going to work, coming home. I've got to pull myself together and *do* something.' And then it struck me that what I needed to do was move.

My son Peter was living and working in Portsmouth. 'Why don't you come down and stay with me while you have a look around the area and see what work's available?' he suggested. So that's what I did. Fortunately, I found a job quickly, as an accountant for a firm of solicitors, and shortly afterwards I moved into a little three-bedroom house in the Hampshire village of Stubbington, between Portsmouth and Southampton.

Peter was wonderful. He helped me move in and drove me into Southampton to buy some things I needed for the house. A couple of days later, though, I decided that one of the items I'd bought wasn't quite right and I wanted to return it. Suddenly, I was almost overwhelmed by a sense of panic: I couldn't remember what road we'd taken to Southampton, where we'd parked, how we'd got from wherever we'd parked to the shops. I felt completely helpless and simply couldn't imagine doing it all on my own. How was I going to manage to do *everything* on my own for the rest of my life?

I kept remembering how I'd felt after I'd left Roy, when I'd been struggling to cope and had fallen gradually deeper into what had seemed to be a bottomless pit of hopelessness and despair. 'That isn't going to happen this time, Sheila,' I told myself firmly. 'You *can* cope on your own. You've done it before and you can do it again. And anyway, you're not the same person now that you were then: being loved by Austin has made you stronger.'

So I drove the car to Southampton, parked in a multistorey car park and returned the unwanted item to the shop where I'd bought it. Then I had a cup of coffee, looked at the new clothes that had just arrived in the women's department of Tyrrell & Green, and drove home again, feeling that I'd taken the first small but significant step on the road towards accepting my new life alone.

In fact, I enjoyed the life that developed for me while I

was living in Stubbington. I met a lot of very nice people, made some good friends and got a wonderful Dachshund puppy, which remained an important part of my life for the next eleven years.

I left the solicitors' firm after a while and applied for a job at a small company of accountants. It's a bit late in my life to be making a clean breast of it now, but I got that job under false pretences, because I lied about my age. It was a friend who 'put me up to it'. She assured me that I didn't look my full fifty-something years and that, 'Many people won't read the rest of your CV once they see your age. You could certainly get away with knocking five years off it, or more.' So that's what I did, although I'd like to think that even if that helped me to get an interview, it was my past track record and natural talent for numbers that actually won me the job!

Then, one day, Peter suggested that I should start working for myself. Having trained as a graphic designer, he was working with the business telephone directory Yellow Pages and had done an advertisement for a woman who did accountancy from home. It sounded like a good idea, so I bought a computer, organized a work space in the house and became a self-employed accountant.

After Austin died, I sometimes used to think, 'I'll be glad when I'm sixty and I can retire.' When the day arrived, however, I was working part-time, doing hours that suited me and earning a good income. Retirement didn't seem like such an attractive proposition after all.

When you lose someone you love, you go through a period of believing that you'll never be happy again. I spent less than a quarter of my life with Austin: it was the best quarter, and I'll always miss him. Twenty-seven years after he died, I still think about him a dozen times a day. Sometimes I remember something about him that makes me laugh, and sometimes I miss him so much I just want to sit down and cry.

Gradually, though, my life without him settled into a pleasant, comfortable routine. Peter got married and had two lovely little girls, Harriet and Clarissa. Sometimes, they'd come to stay with me at weekends and we'd do dressing up and art together and play games. Pat and Chris had started a business that was doing very well. They lived with their two wonderful children in Epsom, and I'd go and visit them there, as well as seeing them when they came to stay in their caravan just along the coast from Portsmouth at Bracklesham Bay.

Everything was going along nicely, and then I made what turned out to be a very stupid mistake – I allowed myself to be persuaded by two friends who lived in Cambridgeshire to move so that I'd be near them.

19

I'd had a good life on the south coast. The village of Stubbington was a close-knit community. There was always
something going on there and I'd made a lot of friends. In
Cambridgeshire, things didn't really work out as I'd hoped
and I found it very hard to settle.

After the move, I worked as an accountant for a man
who owned a hardware shop in a nearby village. He kept
inviting me to go to his church. 'It's a Baptist church,' he
told me — at least a dozen times. 'Everyone there is very
friendly. I think you'd like it. Why don't you come?' I knew
he was trying to be kind and thought it would be a way of
helping me to make friends. But having realized that I'd
made a very bad decision by moving away from the con-
tented life I'd built up for myself, I'd lost my confidence.
The thought of meeting new people made me anxious,
and I wasn't interested in going to any church. Eventually
though, having run out of even vaguely plausible excuses,
I accepted his invitation.

The church was just a five-minute walk away from
where I was living. Before I left the house, I took a very
deep breath and checked in the mirror to make sure I
didn't look as panic-stricken as I felt. When I arrived at
the church hall, I'd taken only half a dozen steps across its
wooden floor when a broadly smiling woman greeted me

effusively saying, 'Hello! How nice to see you. It *is* good of you to come.'

'Oh no,' I thought, 'she's mistaken me for someone else. How embarrassing! I knew this was a bad idea.' But I was wrong: everyone was equally friendly and welcoming and before long I was chatting to people as though I'd known them for years.

I started going to the Baptist church regularly after that and I met people there whose friendship helped to dispel the terrible loneliness I'd felt since I'd moved to the area. As well as making friends, I was finally given an answer to the question about the Holy Spirit I'd asked all those years earlier when the local vicar came to the home for unmarried mothers to talk to us, selectively, about religion.

I was in my late sixties when I was baptized, in water that had been specially warmed in deference to my advanced years! My baptism was a wonderful event, which was witnessed by many members of my family. Afterwards we had a huge, very happy lunch in the church hall, which is where I also subsequently celebrated my seventieth birthday. So something good did come out of the mistake I'd made in moving.

After a while though, for one reason and another, I decided to return to the south coast, where I'd gone after Austin died and where I'd eventually been happy. I bought a flat in a very pleasant block of retirement flats and on 13 August 2004 I moved back down to the south coast, which is where I still live today.

Peter lives in Canada now. Sadly, his marriage didn't turn out as well as Pat's did to Chris, although he's found someone else and he's content. I haven't seen his daughters since the divorce. Their mother rang one day to tell me they didn't want to see me any more. I still don't understand why that happened: whenever they came to stay with me we always had so much fun. That phone call was nine years ago and those little girls – my granddaughters – will be young women now. It makes me very sad to think that I don't know them.

I've been to Toronto to stay with Peter a few times, but I doubt if I'll go there again: the prospect of such a long journey is daunting when you're in your eighties. Not that I feel old, most of the time. I'm a firm believer in the idea that you're only as old as you allow yourself to think you are. Unfortunately, it's a concept that parts of my body don't seem to be familiar with, particularly my back, which quite clearly thinks it's at least twenty years older than my chronological age; and I know it would complain loudly and persistently if I sat for hours in an aeroplane.

I have a wonderful relationship with my daughter Pat. Her husband, Chris, had a stroke when he was just a young man in his forties, so they've had some problems to deal with. But they've dealt with them and they're happy together and love each other.

Now that I'm back living on the south coast and getting a bit less mobile than I used to be, I don't get up to see them and their children – now grown-up – very often. But Pat phones me regularly and we talk about everything under the sun. She's a wonderful daughter; I don't know what I'd do without her. I thank God every single day for the day she was born, and for Peter, too.

When I became pregnant with Pat I didn't know what lay ahead for me. Of course, no one knows that. However, early on in their lives, most people have at least potential options, whereas being unmarried and pregnant in 1950 instantly decimated those options for me. After Pat was born, I didn't expect any young man to be interested in me and I certainly didn't expect that I would ever get married.

Looking back now, from the vantage point afforded by being the great age of eighty-one, I can see things I couldn't see when I was young. Sometimes, it's like watching a film and wanting to scream at the protagonist, 'No! Don't do that. Go back. Take another path. Can't you see that that way it will all end in tears?' And yet there are other things I wouldn't change for all the world.

My mother had several miscarriages as well as the full-term pregnancies that resulted in the birth of children she didn't want. It was almost as if she didn't understand the connection between having sex and becoming pregnant! I did though, and I took a risk when I had sex with Pat's father. The emotional and psychological reasons for not saying 'No' to him aren't any excuse; they're just an explanation that I couldn't see at the time.

I married Roy for the same reasons of low self-esteem. I did love him, although I think part of the reason *why* I loved him was that he seemed to love me despite the fact that I was an unmarried mother, and because he was apparently fond of Pat, something that was very important to me.

And then there was Austin, the man I adored. I wish I'd met him sooner, although I'll always be grateful that I met him at all and that he loved me, purely and simply. It was Austin who finally silenced the voice of my mother that had always whispered in my head, 'You're not good enough.' What Austin gave me was love. Perhaps paradoxically, a man I didn't love and another man I fell out of love with gave me the most important things in my life – my children and my grandchildren.

I've made many mistakes during the last eighty-one years; but there are just two really big ones for which I won't ever forgive myself. One was sending Peter to live with his father when he was just a little boy and I should have kept him with me. The other was not intervening when Roy treated Pat so unkindly.

There's no point now trying to explain or excuse sending Peter away. At the time, everything that had happened before in my life, all the unhappiness and insecurities that I'd repressed and never faced, seemed to be catching up with me. I was losing the battle I'd always fought against self-doubt: I truly did believe that I wasn't the best person to take care of Peter and that he needed to be with his father, whom he loved. Peter was a lovely little boy and he's grown into a wonderful, sweet-natured man. We've had our differences of opinion over the years, but I've never for one moment stopped loving him. I was wrong to send Peter to live with his father. Not because

Roy didn't love him – he did; but because it must have seemed to Peter that I didn't want him. And that wasn't ever true.

It was thanks to the love and persistent encouragement of her husband, Chris, that Pat finally overcame the damage Roy did to her self-estecm. How could I have allowed Roy to treat her the way he did? How could I have stood by and let her be bullied and hurt by him, particularly when I knew from my own experience as a child what terrible damage that can do?

By the time I left Roy, Pat's childhood was over and the opportunity to make it happy for her – as I'd always been so determined to do – had been missed. I did try to make it up to her, but there are some things that it's just too late to put right: even creating a better future doesn't cancel out a destructive past. In view of everything that happened, it seems remarkable to me that she's done so well with her life, has had such a happy marriage and has – with Chris – given her own children the secure, loving, two-parent childhood I wished for her and Peter.

When I think that I might have given Pat up for adoption and never seen her again after I left the home for unmarried mothers and their babies, I feel physically sick. I think Pat has always known I love her; I hope Peter has too.

Someone asked me recently what I was going to be doing on Mothers' Day and it made me think about what that day means to me. I certainly had precious little to thank my own mother for and, from the very limited contact I had with Grandma Pearson, it's possible that my mother had similar feelings about her. And then I realized that, for me, it's the day when I thank God for my children and for allowing me the very special blessing of *being* a mother – which is something I'm grateful for every day of every year of my life.

Acknowledgements

When I submitted my 2000 words to the Saga competition I also wrote a covering letter. That letter was read by Penguin's commissioning editor Daniel Bunyard, who immediately got in touch with me and asked me to write more – about my stay in the home for unmarried mothers and my experiences of having a child 'out of wedlock' in the 1950s. I did what Daniel asked and his enthusiasm and support helped me throughout the whole process. What he also suggested was that I should work with a ghost-writer, and thus I got to know Jane Smith. Jane put my story into words and I could not have managed it half as well as she did. My very grateful thanks to both of you.

JEFF PEARCE

A POCKETFUL OF HOLES AND DREAMS

The poor boy who made his fortune . . . not just once but twice.

Little Jeff Pearce grew up in a post-war Liverpool slum. His father lived the life of an affluent gentleman whilst his mother was forced to steal bread to feed her starving children. Life was tough and from the moment Jeff could walk he learned to go door to door, begging rags from the rich, which he sold down the markets. Leaving school at the age of fourteen, he embarked on an extraordinary journey, and found himself, before the age of thirty, a millionaire.

Then, after a cruel twist of fate left him penniless, he, his wife and children were forced out of their beautiful home.

With nothing but holes in his pockets, Jeff had no alternative but to go back down the markets and start all over again. Did he still have what it took? Could he really get back everything he had lost?

A Pocketful of Holes and Dreams is the heartwarming true story of a little boy who had nothing but gained everything and proof that, sometimes, rags can be turned into riches . . .

CHRISTINE MARION FRASER

BLUE ABOVE THE CHIMNEYS

The wild childhood of a Glasgow tenement urchin

Born during the Second World War in Glasgow, Christine Fraser was her mother's eighth child. Growing up with her siblings in a tiny flat, learning to avoid her hardworking, hard-drinking one-eyed father, making a menace of herself in the streets along with the other urchins, Christine lived an impoverished life but never once cared. Until she was struck down by a terrible illness.

Suddenly, her wild days of childhood were over. A long spell in hospital completely changed her life. Now she found herself dependent on others for so many of her needs. And on top of that her mother and father died.

Yet Christine was always resourceful and never once looked down. She knew that always there, if you looked hard enough, was some blue up above the chimneys.

MOLLY WEIR

SHOES WERE FOR SUNDAY

'Poverty is a very exacting teacher and I had been taught well'

The post-war urban jungle of the Glasgow tenements was the setting for Molly Weir's childhood. From sharing a pull-out bed in her mother's tiny kitchen to running in terror from the fever van, it was an upbringing that was cemented in hardship. Hunger, cold and sickness was an everyday reality and complaining was not an option.

Despite the crippling poverty, there was a vivacity to the tenements that kept spirits high. Whether Molly was brushing the hair of her wizened neighbour Mrs MacKay, running to Jimmy's chip shop for a ha'penny of crimps or dancing at the annual fair, there wasn't a moment to spare for self-pity. Molly never let it get her down as she and the other urchins knew how to make do with nothing.

And at the centre of her world was her fearsome but loving Grannie, whose tough, independent spirit taught Molly to rise above her pitiful surroundings and achieve her dreams.

IRIS JONES SIMANTEL

FAR FROM THE EAST END

From the dirty streets of the East End to the Welsh countryside, will little evacuee Iris ever find somewhere to belong?

Born in 1938 under threat of looming war, Iris spent her early years playing in the rubble of bombed buildings in Dagenham by day and cowering in a dusty shelter at night. But the hardships of poverty and the dreaded Blitz could not match the pain she felt at her parents' indifference. She prayed that just once her mother would hold her when the bombs rained down. But loneliness only intensified when she was evacuated.

Finding the nurturing home she had always dreamt of in her adopted Welsh parents, she wonders what, when she returns to London after the war, will be waiting for her. Will she ever be able to love her philandering father, depressive mother and an angry, bullying brother? Will her family even survive? Or will she have to look farther afield for the affection she so longs for?

'A mesmerizing life story told by an extraordinary 74-year-old with an incredible zest for life' This is Exeter

'A natural and authentic voice, employing comedy, pathos and disarming honesty to depict a hotchpotch of family members' Saga Magazine

He just wanted a decent book to read ...

Not too much to ask, is it? It was in 1935 when Allen Lane, Managing Director of Bodley Head Publishers, stood on a platform at Exeter railway station looking for something good to read on his journey back to London. His choice was limited to popular magazines and poor-quality paperbacks – the same choice faced every day by the vast majority of readers, few of whom could afford hardbacks. Lane's disappointment and subsequent anger at the range of books generally available led him to found a company – and change the world.

'We believed in the existence in this country of a vast reading public for intelligent books at a low price, and staked everything on it'
Sir Allen Lane, 1902–1970, founder of Penguin Books

The quality paperback had arrived – and not just in bookshops. Lane was adamant that his Penguins should appear in chain stores and tobacconists, and should cost no more than a packet of cigarettes.

Reading habits (and cigarette prices) have changed since 1935, but Penguin still believes in publishing the best books for everybody to enjoy. We still believe that good design costs no more than bad design, and we still believe that quality books published passionately and responsibly make the world a better place.

So wherever you see the little bird – whether it's on a piece of prize-winning literary fiction or a celebrity autobiography, political tour de force or historical masterpiece, a serial-killer thriller, reference book, world classic or a piece of pure escapism – you can bet that it represents the very best that the genre has to offer.

Whatever you like to read – trust Penguin.